The Criminal Recidivi

This book describes a large-scale retrospective study of the psychological antecedents of criminal recidivism. Previous work has shown that a variety of measures can predict recidivism but does little to elucidate what actually happens when an experienced offender reoffends after release from prison. In contrast, this study proceeds from the perspective that criminal actions are the result of ongoing psychological processes, and that they can be understood better in this context. Interviews and tests on over 300 men newly returned to prison looked at their problems, emotions, thoughts, and behavior prior to reoffending. The results show a broad range of differences between the recidivists and a comparison group of exoffenders surviving in the community. Moreover, the antecedents for recidivism differed according to the type of new offense, indicating how experiential and environmental details may direct the course of recidivism. The results have substantial implications for release supervision, rehabilitation programs, and the prediction of recidivism, as well as for our theoretical understanding of predatory crime.

Conclusion

Cambridge Studies in Criminology

Editors
Alfred Blumstein, *Carnegie Mellon University*
David Farrington, *University of Cambridge*

The Criminal
Recidivism Process

Edward Zamble
Queen's University at Kingston

Vernon L. Quinsey
Queen's University at Kingston

CAMBRIDGE
UNIVERSITY PRESS

PUBLISHED BY THE PRESS SYNDICATE OF THE UNIVERSITY OF CAMBRIDGE
The Pitt Building, Trumpington Street, Cambridge, United Kingdom

CAMBRIDGE UNIVERSITY PRESS
The Edinburgh Building, Cambridge CB2 2RU, UK
40 West 20th Street, New York, NY 10011-4211, USA
10 Stamford Road, Oakleigh, Melbourne 3166, Australia
Ruiz de Alarcón 13, 28014 Madrid, Spain
Dock House, The Waterfront, Cape Town 8001, South Africa

http://www.cambridge.org

First published 1997
First paperback edition 2001

Printed in the United States of America

Typeface New Baskerville

A catalog record for this book is available from the British Library

Library of Congress Cataloging in Publication data is available

ISBN 0 521 58179 6 hardback
ISBN 0 521 79510 9 paperback

Contents

Illustrations and Tables

Preface

WE BELIEVE THAT the results of this research should be of interest to a variety of correctional practicioners and administrators, as well as to other researchers or specialized students. Therefore, in writing (and rewriting) this volume we have tried very hard to keep it at a level that should be understandable to an intelligent reader, regardless of background. It has proven to be a difficult task. If we omit or oversimplify too much, we may violate the standards of rigorous evidence and lose the confidence of our academic peers. If we complicate things too much with understatements and caveats, we will convince other readers that they are caught in an unrewarding reprocessed graduate thesis (and our theses were done long ago).

We have not succeeded everywhere as well as we would have liked, but we have tried. We vowed to avoid footnotes in the text and managed to break the habit after only one relapse. The single exception, on the first page, kept us comfortable in getting past the initial stages and should do the same for other academics. We have also minimized the listing of inferential statistics, to the point where the average undergraduate ought to be able to work his or her way through them. Some multivariate analyses are included, but they are offset into discrete sections which the less statistically sophisticated reader can skip with a clear conscience; these sections do strengthen our case overall, but they give very much the same message as those with simpler statistics.

We hope that the result is both intellectually and scientifically rigorous and as readable as possible under the circumstances. If we lapse into obscurity, it is our own recidivism, educed by old habits and environmental pressure.

If this work is of value, it is so because our own efforts have been much aided and augmented by various agencies and individuals. We would like to thank Bill Frid, Becky Hooey, and Maria Hooey, who did most of the actual data collection. We are also grateful to Frank Porporino, formerly Director of Research in the Correctional Service of Canada, who gave us the wherewithal to begin the research, and to Dave Robinson and Larry Motiuk of the research branch, who helped in the conduct of the work. The bulk of the funding for this project was provided by a grant from the Social Science and Humanities Research Council of Canada.

We would also like to thank the many individuals in the federal correctional service who actively helped us in making arrangements and in gathering data. Without them we might never have been able to collect enough data to make the study viable. Finally, of course, we would like to thank the men who gave us their time and stories; without them, there would *be* no study.

E. Z.   V. L. Q.   Kingston, Ontario

CHAPTER ONE

Introduction: The Prediction of Criminal Behavior

Static and Dynamic Variables

The prediction of both general and violent criminal recidivism of persons released from correctional institutions has received extensive study (for reviews see Andrews and Bonta, 1994; Blackburn, 1993). This literature indicates that a variety of measures are positively and reliably related to the probability of criminal recidivism.[1] Enough work has been completed to establish a consensus within the correctional research community about the classes of variables that are valid predictors of recidivism, and the degree to which they are related to the criterion behaviors of interest.

Among the best commonly available predictors are youthfulness and number of previous arrests. Other predictors, including age at

[1] There have been a large number of Canadian follow-up studies of released inmates: Andrews and Friesen (1987), Carlson (1973), Gendreau, Grant, and Leipciger (1979a), Gendreau, Madden, and Leipciger (1979b, 1980), Hart, Kropp, and Hare (1988), Malcolm, Andrews, and Quinsey (1993); Mandelzys (1979), Nuffield (1982), Porporino, Zamble, and Higginbottom (1990), Waller (1974), Wormith and Gold-stone (1984), and Zarb (1978). Additional Canadian data come from follow-up studies of released mentally disordered offenders or mixed samples of mental patients and inmates (e.g., Harris, Rice, and Quinsey, 1993; Quinsey and Maguire, 1986; Quinsey, Rice, and Harris, 1995b; Rice, Quinsey, and Houghton, 1990b). American studies include Adams (1983), Barton and Turnbull (1979), Beck and Shipley (1987), Brown, D'Agostino, and Craddick (1978), Gottfredson, Wilkins, and Hoffman (1978), Gottfredson, Mitchell-Herzfeld, and Flanagan (1982), Heilbrun, Heilbrun, and Heilbrun (1978), Holland, Holt, and Brewer (1978), and Rhodes (1986).

first arrest, criminal versatility (variety of offending), alcohol abuse, and low educational attainment, are usually found to be positively but less strongly related to recidivism rates. Although there are conflicting findings on the use of institutional behavior in predicting postrelease recidivism, escape and escape attempts have always been found to be related to higher recidivism rates. Measures of antisociality, such as psychopathy (Hare, 1991), yield higher correlations with recidivism than single predictors commonly available in institutional files, although they are more expensive to collect.

It is of interest that the types of predictors found useful in predicting recidivism among convicted offenders are very similar to those that have been found to predict the initiation of criminal behavior in longitudinal studies of relatively unselected samples of children and adolescents. For example, Farrington (1995) describes those from the Cambridge Study in Delinquent Development as previous antisocial behavior, impulsivity, low intelligence and attainment, family criminality, poverty, and poor parental child-rearing behavior.

Given the predictive usefulness of single variables, one would expect that combining a variety of predictors would be a way of increasing reliability and therefore predictive accuracy. This has been done with good results by several investigators in various jurisdictions. Typically, a mixture of measures are given weightings determined by the degree to which they each singly differentiate between recidivists and nonrecidivists, and the weightings are simply summed, following the pioneering work of Burgess (1925). Essentially, this is an actuarial method, using the best available discriminators, without consideration of how or why they predict future criminal activity, although the nature of the predictors may have theoretical implications (Quinsey, 1995).

A variety of such instruments are available. Those developed in Canada include the general recidivism and violent recidivism scales of Nuffield (1982), the Level of Supervision Inventory (Andrews et al., 1986a; Bonta and Motiuk, 1985), and the Violence Risk Appraisal Guide (Harris et al., 1993). Comparable scales have been developed in the United States, including most notably the Salient Factor Score used in the federal prison system (Hoffman, 1983; Hoffman and Beck, 1985), and scales used in several states, for example, Iowa (Fischer, 1981), Wisconsin (Baird, 1981), and Illinois (Fowler and Jones, 1982).

Although each of these scales predicts recidivism far better than chance, there is still room for improvement (Rice and Harris, 1995). As a rough generalization, we may say that the level of correct prediction is usually about halfway between chance and perfection, a level that is better than clinical prediction and good enough to justify the current use of actuarial scales in many jurisdictions for either classification or release decisions.

However, with few exceptions, the success of predicting violent recidivism has been much lower than that for general recidivism because the probability of violent recidivism is low in most circumstances (e.g., Gabor, 1986; Monahan, 1981; Nuffield, 1982; Quinsey, 1980, 1984; Quinsey and Maguire, 1986; Steadman and Cocozza, 1974; Thornberry and Jacoby, 1979) unless long follow-ups are completed with serious offenders (e.g., Harris et al., 1993). Given the relative infrequency of serious offences against the person, most studies, even those with large samples, essentially examine predictors of robbery, breaking and entering, and other property crimes, not interpersonal violence. This welcome rarity of postrelease violence means that efforts to predict it over relatively short follow-up periods inevitably result in unacceptably high false positive rates (Villeneuve and Quinsey, 1995), although the accuracy of predicting violent and general recidivism is about the same, at least for some actuarial instruments (Rice and Harris, 1995). At present, the extent to which variables that uniquely predict violent crimes against the person add to the predictive accuracy of those that predict general recidivism or nonviolent crime is unclear (Holland et al., 1978; Mandelzys, 1979).

The literature deals almost exclusively with static or "tombstone" predictors, that is, measures of personal history such as age, offence history, or previous substance abuse. In general, these predictors are defined by past events, and they are subject to change only slowly and incrementally (e.g., by an increase in the number of previous offences) if at all. In contrast, even at the beginning of a prison term, correctional program managers require information about factors that are modifiable to a greater degree and over relatively shorter times in order to plan interventions effectively. At the end of the term, what is needed is specific information about the risk for future offences presented by each particular offender, and the ways in which that risk can best be monitored or lowered by supervision. However, at best the empirical follow-up literature can only inform authorities about which classes of offenders should receive the most intensive supervision or interventions, rather than what the nature of the supervision or intervention should be for each individual, and current techniques are far from being able to specify what events after release trigger recidivism.

This gap between the needs of program managers and the static focus of the empirical literature is most readily apparent in the prediction of violent reoffending among mentally disordered offenders. Mentally disordered offenders are typically dealt with by mental health professionals working in psychiatric hospital systems that explicitly espouse a treatment-rehabilitation model. Nevertheless, of 28 follow-up studies of released mentally disordered offenders identified in a review of this literature (Quinsey, 1988), 25 employed only static predictors, and only three (of which two were essentially pilot investigations) attempted to predict recidivism from measures of therapeutic change.

Thus, previous prediction methods are limited because their reliance on static measures ensures that they fail to provide the sort of specific information that is necessary for effective correctional practice. For the vast majority of offenders, the question is not whether they will be released, but when. If the conditions of imprisonment or the time of release are determined on the basis of static historical factors at the beginning of a sentence, then imprisonment will provide little incentive for inmates to change their current behavior patterns.

Thus, the bulk of the follow-up literature can provide very little information to guide correctional workers in choosing appropriate programs for offenders or in making decisions based upon offender change. The paucity of well-designed intervention evaluation studies carried out on prison populations only exacerbates this problem. All of the above leads to the conclusion that we must redirect attention from the general determinants of recidivism (except to identify high-risk groups for concentrated attention) to questions of how to reduce or prevent it in the community.

We are not the first to arrive at this conclusion. In the preface to Waller's (1974) book on prison releasees, Edwards (p. vii) states: "What is called for is a major realignment of the time and energies of those engaged in the fields of correction and related organizations toward the alleviation of those problems associated with employment, family and community relationships, and alcoholism which are at the root of most failures following release." Although this statement contains assumptions about the specific causes of recidivism, it correctly emphasizes the role of postrelease factors.

What is needed is a better understanding of the role of current factors in the causation of new offences. Criminal recidivism can result from unresolved problems within a released offender that could have been addressed during a period of imprisonment, or it could be a consequence of new environmental or offender problems occurring after release. How much either or both of these occur in any given case, or across all cases, is both empirically and conceptually unclear (cf. Mandelzys, 1979).

What is needed is a research focus on the specific contemporaneous determinants of recidivism. This is not to say that we should discard the information we already have on static predictors of release failure. Historical factors, especially those measured early in life, will retain an important place among the determinants of criminal misconduct, both for understanding its origins in an individual and as predictors.

However, at present we have little knowledge of other determinants. We do not know much about what actually happens just before and during the occurrence of recidivism. Several sorts of events are of interest here, all of them dynamic as opposed to the static factors emphasized in the literature, in the sense that they are at least potentially changeable over the time periods of interest. There are first relatively stable but still alterable behavior patterns of offenders, such as ways of coping, antisocial attitudes and values, and criminal socialization. These may have been strongly influenced by historical events and therefore are correlated with and predictable from static variables. However, future changes may be independent of the original causes and are therefore neither correlated with nor predictable from static measures. If these behavioral and cognitive states are the real mediators of reoffending, then direct measurement of them will be more powerful than the indirectly related static measures, especially after some intervention aimed at inducing change has occurred.

In addition to generalized personal characteristics of the offender, we assume that behavior is also strongly influenced by specific dynamic local antecedents, both responses within the offender and identifiable events in the external environment. These include passing emotional experiences, thoughts, perceptions, and many, many other events that include most of the range of ongoing psychological processes entering actively into the choice of behaviors. Such events are not only dynamic, but often labile or transitory. Although they may be more difficult to capture, describe, and quantify than static indicators, contemporary explanations of behavior processes lead one to expect that they are critically involved and important when recidivism occurs.

There have been some attempts to specify how the manner in which offenders interact with their current environment is related to future offending (Zamble and Porporino, 1988), and it has been shown that one can predict recidivism using measures of current behavior as well as from static variables (Porporino et al., 1990). There is also evidence that events occurring after release affect recidivism. For example, Motiuk and Porporino (1989) found that adding postrelease ratings of parole officers to the SIR scale (based on Nuffield's [1982] general prediction scale) increased predictive accuracy. However, the information provided by such previous work is only fragmentary, even though it is encouraging.

Thus, we need to know a great deal more about what sorts of mechanisms are involved in recidivism, and we also need to ascertain how they express themselves in the sequence of events leading to new criminal offences. In short, what is called for is an investigation into the *process* of recidivism. Rather than a continued or even an enhanced search for static predictors associated with recidivism, it might be more productive to work to construct a plausible model that incorporates factors that have proven empirically to be predictive.

To this end, then, inclusion of a variety of dynamic antecedent measures is essential. The value of the resultant model will depend on how well it provides an analysis of recidivism in the context of contemporary understanding of psychological and behavioral processes, as well as how effective it proves in predicting recidivism and in directing preventive measures.

Supervision after Release

One area that should both inform and be informed by this enterprise is the effectiveness of supervision under early release. Unfortunately, the literature on the effectiveness of parole and mandatory supervision is quite small, and it is replete with methodological problems (Nietzel and Himelein, 1987). In summarizing the best-executed research on the issue of supervision versus no supervision, Gottfredson et al. (1982) conclude that "First, none of the studies indicates a lasting effect of parole supervision beyond the period of supervision itself. Second, the research seems to indicate an effect of parole supervision on recidivism during the course of the supervision, particularly in the initial period of release. Third, the effect indicated by the research does not appear to be very large."

The limited effectiveness of supervision follows from our arguments above, for it is difficult to know what sorts of parole programs to develop in the absence of good information on the antecedents of release failure. With better knowledge about the antecedent conditions of recidivism, parole authorities, or even offenders themselves, could take actions to avoid the commission of new criminal acts.

What do we know about the antecedents of parole failure? With respect to general recidivism, Waller (1974) found that lack of employment, undesirable associates, fighting, not seeing one's children, and frequent drinking predicted reoffending. Hart et al. (1988) similarly observed that instability in both employment and relationships during the follow-up period predicted reoffending. Shover's (1996) ethnographic study of persistent thieves reveals a similar picture. The typical lifestyle of these men can be best described as "life as a party" in which good times are sought with few concerns for external obligations or commitments. In the language of evolutionary psychology, this enjoyment of the moment accompanied by alcohol and drug abuse, variety in sexual partners, risk taking, and intermale competition and aggression can be described as high mating effort (as opposed to parental investment).

Determinants of sexual reoffending among 136 child molesters and 64 rapists have been examined in more detail by Pithers et al. (1988). Nearly 90% of the sex offenders reported experiencing strong emotional states before the commission of a new sex offence: 94% of the rapists reported feeling anger, usually occasioned by interpersonal conflict; 46% of the child molesters reported experiencing anxiety, and 38% reported depression; these emotional states appeared to be related to social disaffiliation. The chain leading to relapse seemed to begin with negative affect leading to paraphilic sexual fantasies, then cognitive distortions, and, finally, passive planning just before the offence.

Frisbie (1969), based on 550 interviews of 311 child molesters under supervision, concluded that, besides alcohol abuse, factors predicting recidivism were "the desire for and selection of physically immature children as sexual objects, unorthodox ethical values, and grave difficulties in establishing meaningful relationships with adult females on a mature basis" (p. 223). The similarities between Frisbie's observations and those of Pithers et al. (fantasies, disaffiliation, and cognitive distortion) are striking. Planning and behavioral rehearsal as antecedents to serious sexual offences have also been noted by MacCulloch et al. (1983). It is of interest in the present context that Frisbie was surprised at how much her interviewees would disclose to a project interviewer; because of their home visits, the research team were often aware of impending relapse before the parole authorities.

In summary, it may be said that previous studies of the antecedents of parole failure have not produced findings detailed or unambiguous enough for actual application to the development of supervisory policies. Most of the work considered above has not dealt with serious offenders against persons (that is, those of most concern) and has implicitly treated offenders as a homogeneous population. Some studies of better-defined groups of released offenders, such as rapists and child molesters, do include consideration of the ongoing process, but they have not included comparison groups of other kinds of offenders and seldom offenders of the same type who did not reoffend.

Clearly, a great deal more work is required to develop the knowledge required to inform parole supervision policy. We envision an extended and comprehensive inquiry, the centerpoint of which would probably be a large-scale long-term follow-up of offenders using both prerelease and postrelease data to predict recidivism of various kinds. The final step would be an evaluation study to determine whether recidivism can be reduced to a meaningful degree by interventions designed to alter the dynamic elements, both general and specific, that are found to predict it.

However, such studies would be very expensive, and it would be premature to undertake such ambitious enterprises before carefully laying out the conceptual and empirical underpinnings. To provide information for this conceptual effort, the principal antecedents must be identified first. For a first approximation at variable selection, we can use a number of criteria, including the demands of a theoretical model, continuity with previous work on prison populations (Zamble and Porporino, 1988), ease of measurement, known relationships with parole outcome, and evidence that changes in the variable produced by interventions are related to lower recidivism (e.g., Ross, Fabiano, and Ewles, 1988). These were the bases for initial selection in the study to be reported here. Once the precursors have been identified, and their role clarified, reliable and practical measures for field use must be developed before the major validation studies.

Thus, the research described in this monograph was the first step in developing a model of recidivism as an ongoing psychological process. As such, we expected that new criminal offences result from an interaction between internal dispositions and external events, so a variety of dynamic factors were included, among them measures of stress, social support, coping skills, substance abuse, supervisory and intervention variables, and affective states.

In addition, an attempt was made to deal with the problem of base rates, to put previous results into perspective. What are we to make, for example, of the finding (Pithers et al., 1988) that most sex offenders report negative affect before they committed their offence? What is the base rate of negative affect among released offenders of any type, and is it related to the probability or type of reoffending? Perhaps more to the point, we are not even sure of the base rate of negative affect among demographically similar members of the general population. The observation that negative affect precedes sexual reoffending, therefore, may be correct but uninformative. For these reasons, two types of comparisons were included in the research design. The first is between reoffenders and those who successfully adapt to the community after release; the second is among offenders who commit different types of crimes.

Coping and Relapse Theory

Two previous lines of investigation guided development of this project and the way it attempted to describe the interaction between the offender and his environment. The first direction comes from a large-scale Canadian study intended to specify how offenders interact with their environment, and especially how they cope with their problems (Zamble and Porporino, 1988). Although it was primarily designed to study the behavior of male inmates in prison, the primary study also included data on problems experienced by inmates before imprisonment, and the resulting coping attempts.

We can define coping responses as a person's attempts to deal with a perceived problem situation. In the case of offenders, there was no evidence that the problems encountered outside of prison were distinctive in kind or in severity from the ordinary challenges that most people encounter. However, their ways of dealing with these situations were at best ineffective and often exacerbated the original problems.

In addition, there was evidence of an association between this disastrously poor level of coping and retrospective or prospective measures of criminal behavior. For example, there was a significant negative correlation between previous criminal history and coping efficacy. Similarly, future recidivism could be predicted using several measures of the coping process, and the accuracy of prediction was in the same range as that for commonly used actuarial scales (Porporino et al., 1990).

Results of this sort originally led to the formulation of a "coping-criminality" hypothesis (Zamble and Porporino, 1988) linking the repetition of criminal behavior to inadequate coping responses. It was hypothesized that offenders are unable to successfully recognize and resolve their problems, especially chronic situations such as strain in interpersonal relationships. One of the consequences is a considerable amount of stress, during which the person either strikes out blindly or chooses a maladaptive, often criminal, response as a misguided coping effort. A problem for this analysis is the choice of criminal behavior rather than some other form of maladaptation, but it it also known that a variety of generalized behaviors are common among chronic offenders, for example, a large amount of time spent socializing in a diffuse network of casual (mostly criminal) acquaintances, and one may argue that these combine with distinctive criminal cognitions and other factors to channel the results of poor coping into renewed criminal activity.

The case for the role of coping in criminal recidivism has been strengthened by evidence from some associated studies. It has been shown that the efficacy of coping in prison among female prisoners is comparable to the poor levels among males (Loucks and Zamble, 1994). In contrast, the level of coping ability in a noncriminal sample is considerably different from that in offender populations, with very little overlap (Hughes and Zamble, 1993).

Whether it is correct in detail, the coping-criminality hypothesis is supported by data, and some portion of it is very likely veridical. It represents a practical specification of the interaction of the individual offender and his environment and points to the role of particular features of that interaction in determining new criminal actions. However, although it can point to the origins of a breakdown into renewed criminal behavior, the coping explanation in itself is still vague and incomplete in terms of describing what happens after coping resources fail.

This leads us to appeal to a second line of research that concentrates on the events occurring in a breakdown process. Marlatt and Gordon (1985) have proposed a model in which relapse into addictive behaviors is viewed as a result of several factors. "Relapse" is defined as a "failure to maintain behavior change, rather than a failure to initiate change" (Laws, 1989; Annis and Davis, 1989). Their description of relapse begins with what is essentially a failure to cope effectively, within a model of the coping process that is congruent with the work on coping in prisoners cited above and with commonly used models of coping (e.g., Lazarus and Folkman, 1983).

However, the unique contribution of relapse theory is in its focus on the factors responsible for maintenance of behavioral change – or the failures that result in relapse into addiction. Maintenance is thought to depend on several factors. In addition to coping skills, which determine whether one will enter into a high-risk situation, thoughts and cognitions play an important role. In a high-risk situation, individuals make a cognitive appraisal of their ability to cope with the situation. These assessments of self-efficacy are important because they determine subsequent action. For example, if the person decides that he cannot cope with the situation, negative affect and cognitions of hopelessness may ensue, greatly magnifying the chance of a relapse. Thus, the expectation of being able to cope with a difficult situation in itself enhances the chances of coping successfully. In addition, motivation is important as an essential condition for success, while such things as social pressure can strongly increase risks.

For many, the processes involved are automatic and have never been consciously scrutinized. Thus, people may not be aware of the choices, decisions, and expectations that precede and accompany their habitual behaviors. From their perspective, the behaviors or high-risk situations just seem to happen. By its analysis of the sequences of events involved, relapse theory attempts to identify the critical points and to give people better control at dangerous junctions in their behavioral paths. Thus, clients can be taught to recognize some of the signals of an ensuing relapse, to avoid high-risk situations, and to deal better with minor lapses.

The relapse prevention approach was adopted on the basis of the treatment outcome evaluation literature dealing with schizophrenia, psychopathy, and certain classes of offenders. Detailed narrative reviews of the treatment outcome literature are provided by Rice et al. (1990a) for mentally disordered offenders, by Gottesman (1991) for schizophrenics, by Liberman (1988) for chronic mental patients, and by Kazdin (1987) for antisocial youth. Relapse theory is also compatible with risk management strategies based on actuarial appraisals of risk (Gottfredson et al., 1978; Harris et al., 1993; Quinsey and Walker, 1992; Webster et al., 1994).

Treatment dictated by the relapse prevention approach attempts to increase patients' self-efficacy, coping skills, and motivation. Both general (e.g., self-efficacy) and idiosyncratic aspects of each offender's problem behavior are targeted. Through cognitive (providing insight into the "how" and "why" of offenders' behavior) and behavioral (providing actual experiences of mastery/success) means, offenders are taught new ways of coping that will allow them to break the cycle before they relapse completely: "Relapse prevention relies heavily on the client's ability to learn and to initiate appropriate coping behaviors at the earliest possible point in the relapse process" (Laws, 1989, p. 139). By understanding their behavior, and what led up to it, offenders can learn to plan and rehearse alternative prosocial behaviors.

The problem area for which relapse theory was developed is different in important ways from criminal behavior, so that the details of the criminal recidivism process are probably different from those of addictive relapse. However, it points to the sort of processes that almost certainly occur in any breakdown process. Recidivism can be seen as a relapse process in which the offender falls back into old habitual behavior patterns. Therefore, the principal elements in relapse theory can be used to guide inquiry into the ongoing events in the recidivism process.

Relapse theory is also nicely complementary to the coping-criminality explanation. Although they were formulated quite independently and in different contexts, the two approaches are clearly compatible, and probably even synergistic. Each emphasizes different parts of the determinative process, and they dovetail nicely: Coping theory loses definition when coping mechanisms fail, just at the point where relapse theory begins a close specification of events. More specifically, for the coping-criminality hypothesis, the links between inadequate coping and criminal actions are likely emotional distress and cognitions that either trigger antisocial behavior themselves or defeat the individual's efforts at self-monitoring and self-control. Conversely, within relapse theory, the high-risk situations that lead to relapse into criminal recidivism are produced by inappropriate or inadequate coping behaviors. Together, these two sets of ideas specify the probable events of interest from the occurrence of a challenging situation to the commission of a new offence.

However, even if the model proves entirely correct, a great deal needs to be known before we can specify the behavioral processes involved in precipitating new criminal offences. Although the theoretical perspectives outlined above predict what sort of factors are likely involved, the details of the process have not yet been specified. For example, even if we agree that an offence may be triggered by a dysphoric emotional state, the theory does not specify *which* state. Are different offence patterns associated with different emotional states? If coping failures are involved, how much does the type of problem affect the result, and how much is determined by the individual's particular coping responses?

The present study attempted to deal with these and related questions. We expected that the results would be useful in extending our knowledge of the recidivism process, both theoretically and empirically, and we hoped that they would have important implications for the development of supervisory policies for releasees.

Thus, in summary, the purpose of the research reported here was to begin the development of a model of the criminal recidivism process. More specifically, we focused on the role of a variety of specific antecedents (behavioral, emotional, and cognitive) internal and external to the person, distal and proximal, static and dynamic. For direction in choosing the events of interest for investigation, we drew heavily on previous work in coping and relapse prevention. This allowed us to test the usefulness of the integration of these theoretical perspectives and provided a choice of measures and a structure for inquiry.

CHAPTER TWO

The Study

Setting

The core set of subjects in this study were male prisoners in the Ontario region of the Correctional Service of Canada. From this population, we selected only recent recidivists, defined as those who had previously been imprisoned in Canada and had been returned to prison for a new offence committed within a year of their previous release.

Given the constitutional arrangement that mandates responsibility for prisoners in Canada, assignment to the federal system normally means that offenders have sentences of at least two years, with those assigned shorter sentences going to provincial institutions. However, if an offender commits a new offence while under supervision after release from a federal institution, he is returned to federal custody to serve both the remainder of the original term and the new term.

The Ontario region is the largest in the Canadian federal system, drawing from a population of almost 11,000,000. At the time of the study, it included just over 3,000 federal inmates. All prisoners entering the region were sent initially to a Reception Unit in Millhaven Penitentiary, where they were held until sent to their assigned receiving institution. If they had been in the community for only a short time and under supervision when they reoffended, they were sometimes returned within about two weeks to the institution from which they had been previously released, but usually they were held in the Reception Unit for one to two months.

The Millhaven institution had been originally designed as a maximum-security institution in the early 1970s and still housed approximately 100 maximum-security inmates, but part of it had been designated to serve the reception function, although it had not been extensively renovated for the change. Consequently, the regime on the unit was still very close to maximum security. Inmates had no programs to occupy them during the day, and only limited opportunities to leave their cells for recreation and exercise. Because of an increasingly serious shortage of space, the majority were double bunked in cells built for one person. These conditions probably increased willingness to participate in our study, which provided a few hours out of the cell in conversation with an interested interviewer.

Selection of Recidivist Subjects

New inmates who appeared to meet our primary criterion of a new offence within a year of a previous release were identified shortly after arrival. Because we wanted to concentrate on those who had committed serious new offences while under supervision, we required that the new offence be serious enough in itself to warrant a federal term. For some subjects, the new term actually given was less than two years, although the aggregate sentence including the remainder of the previous term was always at least two years for the men we selected.

We also required that potential subjects had served at least one year in prison on their previous terms, to ensure that their previous criminal histories were serious as well as their new crimes. In practice, complete records were not available at the time of selection to indicate previous release from provincial institutions, and men in this category were probably underrepresented, because the previous release for over 90% of our recidivist subjects had been from federal custody.

We recruited a total of 311 subjects according to their most serious new offences: any type of assault against persons (including homicide), robbery and armed robbery, and nonviolent property crimes, primarily breaking and entering or theft. Offences involving rape were included within the violent assault category, but we screened out most other sex offenders, such as those involved in pedophilia and incest, because the amount of violence was impossible to assess from the information available.

Subjects were selected with the intention of having roughly equal numbers in each of the three groups. Given the numbers of potential subjects who arrived, this meant that the selection ratio was somewhat lower for the property offenders than for the others. Thus, subjects were randomly selected from new arrivals within each category, but the aggregate sample does not accurately represent the system population or even the set of new arrivals. The distribution of subjects across groups and new offences can be seen in Table 2.1.

In the ordinary routine, prisoners were seen by a Case Management Officer upon arrival at the institution. Their institutional assignment was then discussed (and sometimes decided upon) in a staff meeting, normally within a week after arrival. Most potential subjects were selected by a research assistant attending these meetings, on the basis of the information available at the time. Possible subjects were selected in the order in which they were discussed in the meetings, an order usually determined by matters of administrative convenience unrelated to inmates' characteristics. The number chosen varied according to the number who could be interviewed within the following week or so. A minority of subjects were chosen from lists of new inmates given to the researchers, from which selections were made after consultation with staff regarding their suitability according to our selection criteria.

Potential subjects were excluded if they exhibited active psychoses, if their command of English was not sufficient to enable them to understand the interview, or if they were considered by staff as unstable and presenting a physical danger to an interviewer. Three subjects were later dropped from the study when clear psychotic behavior became apparent during their interviews, such as the insistence by one that he was possessed by the devil. To our knowledge, no others were dropped because of psychoses before recruitment, probably because staff did not see enough of inmates' behavior before the initial placement meetings for nondisruptive psychotic ideation or behavior to become apparent, so the three who were dropped were probably all of those excluded on this criterion. Given the selection process, it is not possible to say how many were excluded by the other criteria, but the total exclusions were certainly less than 5% of all potential subjects.

Table 2.1. *Subject groups and new offences*

Offence category	Number	Percent[a]
Homicide (murder, manslaughter)	4	1.3
Aggravated assault	12	3.5
Assault	68	21.9
Sexual assault (rape)	16	5.2
Sexual assault (pedophilia)	2	0.6
Robbery and armed robbery	100	32.2
Breaking and entering	64	20.6
Theft, other property	42	13.5
Fraud	3	1.0
Groups		
Assault	102	
Robbery	100	
Property	109	
Nonrecidivists	36	

[a] Nonrecidivists are excluded.

Once they were selected, potential subjects were approached by one of the researchers to enlist their cooperation. The study was described to them, and they were assured confidentiality. If they agreed to participate, they signed a consent form, and an interview was scheduled.

In addition to the 311 completed subjects, there were only 12 refusals, approximately 4% of those approached. This acceptance rate is better than anticipated; as mentioned earlier, it may have been because the study offered a respite from the routine confinement in the Reception Unit. The data-gathering period began in the fall of 1990 and continued until early in 1993, in total about 2½ years.

Nonrecidivist Subjects

In addition to the primary sample of recidivists, a comparison group comprised men who had lived in the community for a period after release from prison without having incurred new charges. We required that they had served at least a year in prison before their release, and that they had some criminal history even before the last imprisonment. The minimum survival period was originally defined as one year, but in practice the criterion was relaxed because of the difficulty of finding suitable candidates.

The correctional system does not maintain lists of forwarding addresses for offenders who have completed their entire sentence, and there seemed to be no practical way to obtain any reasonably unbiased sample of such men. However, by correctional policy, prisoners are released to the community after they have served two-thirds of their sentences, unless there is documented evidence that they present an imminent danger to the community on release, a provision that was very uncommonly invoked at the time of the study. During this final third of the sentence, they were under the supervision of the National Parole Service. The same agency also supervised those released early on parole after serving less than the mandatory portion of their terms.

Therefore, to obtain names of possible subjects, we contacted parole offices in three districts. They agreed to search their caseloads for individuals who met our criteria, to give potential subjects a very short description of the study, and to tell them that they would be paid twenty dollars for their time. If a supervisee agreed to participate, his name and telephone number were given to us, and an appointment scheduled. It is impossible to calculate the proportion of potential subjects who did agree to take part, because parole officers did not report back to us on this. However, informal reports indicated that there were very few refusals from among those who were approached.

Unfortunately, the number recruited was still less than we desired, for several reasons. For one, we were limited to those under supervision and had no access to men who had successfully completed relatively short periods of supervision, even if they maintained lawful conduct afterwards. Second, there was much attrition because of reoffending. (In one of the parole offices, we were allowed to search the caseload ourselves to obtain names of those who met our selection criteria, and we selected possible subjects before they had met our survival criterion; when we checked with the supervising authorities two months later to arrange interviews, almost one-third of those selected earlier had been reimprisoned.) Finally, many of those who might have been eligible were living in areas that were too far from our base for our limited travel funds to accommodate. In the end, a total of only 36 were included in the comparison group.

Interview Measures

Once subjects had been recruited, we obtained data on them from several sources. The most important was a structured interview that included questions on a variety of topics. Excerpts from the complete protocol are included as an Appendix.

The first few questions in the interview concern background and historical information, primarily items that are used in the Level of Supervision Inventory or LSI (Andrews, Kiessling, and Kominos, 1983). This instrument was developed to assess offender risk and has been well validated, although, with the exception of Loza and Simourd (1994), most of the research pertaining to its use has been conducted in provincial (Ontario) institutions (Andrews et al., 1986a; Andrews et al., 1986b; Bonta and Motiuk, 1985, 1987, 1990; Motiuk, Bonta, and Andrews, 1986; Motiuk, Motiuk, and Bonta, 1992). In preliminary work, it became clear that questions in the Probation/Parole Conditions and Attitudes/Orientation subscales of the LSI either were inappropriate to our population or could not be scored, so they were dropped, resulting in a 50-item scale instead of the original 58. The LSI is comprised primarily of historical and static information, but it also contains some dynamic items.

We did not expect that offenders would tell or even know why they committed their offence. If truthful, offenders can usually identify what their intent was when they committed a crime; however, they cannot be expected to have a theory that can explain their own criminal behaviors (Quinsey, Reid, and Stermac 1996). Zamble and Porporino (1988) received detailed answers to questions about responses to specific situations but only vague and self-contradictory answers to questions about the purposes of those responses. Similarly, Quinsey et al. (1996) frequently received logically unintelligible and extremely vague answers from offenders to the question "Why did this offence occur?" We expected that offenders could recall and report details of events preceding reoffending well enough to allow an investigator to construct a theory of reoffending, even though they might not be able to correctly identify the determinants themselves.

Therefore, the great majority of questions in the interview for recidivists focused on events during the period in the community preceding the new offence. When a series of new offences had occurred, the reference point was the first that would have resulted in return to prison, even if it was not the most serious of the set.

For aspects of their lives that usually change only slowly, we asked subjects to answer in terms of the six-month period before their new offence. If subjects had not been at liberty for as long as six months, a period as short as one month was used to depict their time in the community. A few had been rearrested even within a month, in which case we omitted their data for the questions concerned.

A variety of questions asked about the subject's lifestyle in the reference period, such as the persons he was living with, employment, and how he spent his time. Interspersed with these were questions about common problem areas, from living accommodations to interpersonal relationships, to see what difficulties each subject had encountered in living outside of prison.

For behaviors that vary more than lifestyle, the focus was on briefer time periods leading up to the new offence. Particular attention was given to subjects' moods, emotions, and substance abuse, all of which we attempted to assess in some detail. Because we expected that these factors would be particularly important as offence precursors and that they might change over time, parallel questions were asked about the final month and about the day or two immediately preceding the new offence.

The last section of the interview concentrated on events in the offence process itself. In addition to looking at the precursors of offences, we wanted to be able to describe the progression of events in the offence, from a person's first passing thought of the possibility to his actually committing the act. This is important for a number of reasons, among them questions about possible intervention. In addition to the timing of the sequence, we wanted to know how much offenders were aware of their impending criminal actions, and what, if anything, they did in response to such intimations. Thus, this section of the interview concentrated on offenders' actions and thoughts about a possible offence before it occurred.

In addition to direct questions, we gave subjects concrete visual images in the form of timelines presented on separate sheets of paper.

Two such timelines were used, as illustrated in Figure 2.1. The first
timeline marks off a series of points from several months before the
offence until its occurrence, allocating the same lengths of line for
short periods close to the offence as for longer periods farther away.
The compression of units backward in time was chosen as analogous
to the way events in memory are compressed in distant time relative to
a pivotal recent event (such as the occurrence of a new crime), rather
than in a more linear fashion. Thus, the telescopic dimension moving
backward from the offence was conceived as a representation of "psychological log units."

Subjects were asked to mark a series of six milestones on the line,
from their first passing thought of a possible offence, to the point of
inevitability, when they had already begun the series of actions in the
offence. The degree of separation between these points indicates the
amount of premeditation, that is, wide dispersion indicates considerable thought and preparation in advance of the offence, whereas a
spontaneous offence appears as a bunching of the points at the end of
the line.

In some cases, subjects reported not having experienced one or
more of the landmarks, for example, they claimed never to have done
any definite planning. In these cases we assumed that events in the
sequence occurred in strictly linear order, so any event in question
could not have been earlier than the event that precedes it in the
sequence, and times were assigned accordingly. For instance, if an
offender reported that his first passing thought of the offence was
within 15 minutes of its occurrence, and that he did no planning or
preparation, then preparatory events that should normally occur between the first casual thought and enactment were scored as also
having occurred in the final 15 minutes before the crime.

The second timeline (or, more properly, set of three timelines) was
more conventional, with equal spaces allotted to each day in the
month preceding the offence. The separate lines were marked
"Events," "Feelings," and "Thoughts." Subjects were asked to indicate significant occurrences of each type that they could remember
from the period, and approximately when they had been experienced.
In this way, we hoped to obtain at least a fragmentary picture of
psychological events that took place during the period.

In general, the strategy for construction of the interview was guided

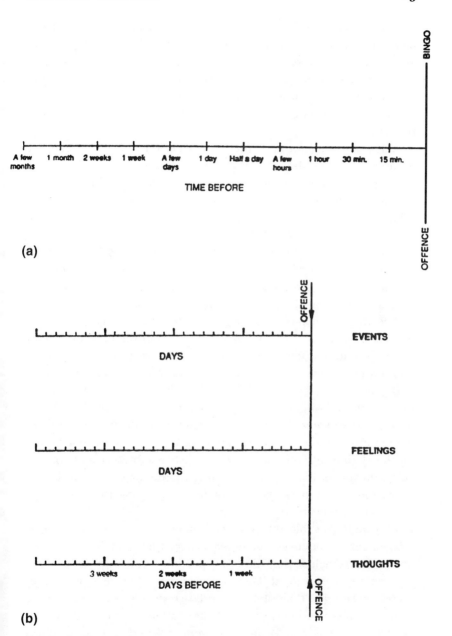

Figure 2.1a, b. The "timelines" used in the interview.

by several objectives. First among these was a desire to arrive at quantifiable information. Whenever possible, the subject was required to give numerical answers. For example, after a panoply of possible problems had been queried, he was asked to rate numerically the seriousness of any problems he had experienced. In other cases, qualitative answers were categorized by the researchers to allow statistical analyses.

At the same time, we attempted to avoid leading questions, in order to capture subjects' thoughts and perceptions as well as possible. Questioning was designed according to the principle of progressive focusing, that is, the first inquiries in a line were open-ended, but the following questions were progressively more specific. Although we often had certain classification schemes in mind, the categorizations were typically done after the answers had been given, so that they did not constrain subjects' answers in advance. Where we did provide specific lists of alternatives to subjects, they were commonly used categories such as emotional states, and the lists were as exhaustive as possible.

The final principle used to guide interview construction was a degree of intentional redundancy. Questions in the most important areas were more often than not repeated in slightly different forms, both for checks on the accuracy of answers and to increase reliability of the overall set of information. For example, questions about emotions in the preoffence period, or about landmarks in the offence process, were essentially duplicated in filling out the timeline. Part of the redundancy was the duplication of information on certain behaviors for slightly different time periods, such as substance abuse in the 48 hours and in the month preceding the offence. This overlap allowed some inferences about possible changes near the time of the offence for labile factors.

It is quite possible that subjects' reports were affected by their subsequent experiences, including arrest, trial, and the return to prison. Nevertheless, they did not report any difficulties in recalling the events we asked about. Their lives had most often changed considerably, shortly after their offences, and such changes should give some distinctiveness to events just before the change of state; moreover, in most cases the events in question were still fairly recent, within a month of the interview. Thus, we are fairly confident that subjects were capable of recalling most of the events covered in the interview.

There is still a problem with retrospective distortion. One might expect some coloring of memories for emotions in light of the dysphoria produced by the return to prison, or some selective cueing of recall for thoughts related to problems experienced. The progressive focusing and the redundancy in the interview were attempts to deal with the problems of retrospection as well as possible, but the data are still open to challenge on these grounds. This problem can be partly circumvented by the comparisons between different subsets of recidivists because the problem ought to be identical across groups of inmates who have committed different types of offences. However, to the extent that it is operative, retrospective bias could change the status of certain measures from predictive to postdictive, that is, measures that might appear to be predictive could have no utility when used in prediction.

More serious is the possibility that subjects either intentionally or unintentionally minimized their culpability. Offenders are known to cast themselves in the best possible light when explaining why they committed their offenses by emphasizing situational and unstable causes as opposed to internal and dispositional factors (e.g., Quinsey et al., 1996). Intentional distortion was dealt with by selecting only subjects who admitted committing the offense and by assuring them of confidentiality. The measures obtained directly from subjects concerned only the relative importance and temporal patterning of particular external causes, so the results should not have been affected by externalizing rationalizations. Nevertheless, we cannot dismiss the possibility that some subjects minimized the amount of such things as premeditation or maximized particular exculpatory factors, such as drinking in the preoffense period. A measure of tendencies toward socially desirable responding was therefore included to assess subjects' tendency to attempt to "look good."

For nonrecidivist subjects in the comparison group, a parallel interview form was used. Of course, given that these men had not committed any identified new offences, questions dealing specifically with the offence sequence or its precursors were inappropriate. Instead, there were questions about thoughts of possible new offences that had not occurred. Similarly, questions about events in the preoffense period used the time of the interview as the reference point in place of the offence.

Questionnaire and File Measures

Subjects were also given a set of questionnaires to gather supplementary information on specific topics. In each case, they were asked to answer in terms of the last month before their new offence – or before the interview for nonrecidivists.

This point of reference raises the same concerns about bias in recollections that were discussed earlier regarding the interview results. However, when we asked about possible recall problems, subjects said that they were easily able to distinguish between their current states and those before the offence. In any case, many of the questionnaires measured specific behaviors that were either general or continuing, such as coping or substance abuse, and these should not be much affected by the timing of their assessment.

The first group of questionnaires included several measures of emotional states. The Beck Depression Inventory (Beck, 1967) is the most widely used self-report scale in the clinical assessment of depression. It has well-established reliability and norms and had been previously used with inmate populations like that used here (Zamble and Porporino, 1988). Similarly, the Spielberger State Anxiety Scale (Spielberger, Gorsuch, and Lushene, 1970) is useful in differentiating patients with anxiety levels of clinical significance; it has good reliability and also has previously been used for prisoners. Finally, anger was measured with Siegel's Multimodal Anger Inventory (1986). This instrument had not to our knowledge been previously used often with a prison population, but it includes a variety of subscales that index aspects of anger, including its sources and expression, and appeared to be well suited to our purposes.

Given the importance of substance abuse in offence etiology, we wanted detailed and normative information on drug and alcohol use. In addition to the data on consumption gathered in the interview, we also wanted information on possible long-term damage and addictive patterns of substance abuse. Therefore, the Alcohol Dependence Scale (Skinner and Horn, 1984) and the Drug Abuse Screening Test (Skinner, 1982) were included.

A third category of scales was intended to measure selected aspects of behavior patterns that have been linked with criminal offending. A new Coping Vignettes Scale was based on findings from Zamble and

Porporino (1988) using a technique explored by Porporino and Zamble (1984). Five problem situations that our previous experience had shown to be common among inmates were included: a disagreement with a spouse over housework, pressure from a supervisor to work harder, running out of money, an invitation to a party on a work night, and loneliness and social isolation after being released from prison.

Subjects were asked to record their likely responses to each. They were also asked to categorize their emotional response, and to rate how serious they thought the situation would be for them and how well they could handle it. The efficacy of coping responses was then rated by one of the investigators on two scales, benefits and risks, that have been previously shown to yield reliable results (Porporino and Zamble, 1984; Zamble and Porporino, 1988). These are normally combined into a single scale of "coping efficacy." (It was expected that coping ability would be strongly linked to outcomes in most circumstances. However, poor coping skills will have no deleterious effect if the environment presents no challenges to be overcome. Therefore, in predictive or comparative analyses we commonly used a measure called "coping adequacy," which is defined as the ratio of coping efficacy to the number of problems experienced.)

A Time Use and Time Framing Scale was devised to measure the lack of planning and anticipation that seems to characterize the lives of many chronic offenders in the community. In the version used in this study there were 30 true-false questions, with half keyed in each direction. The total score is intended to measure planning of time and concern with timeframes outside of the present.

In addition to the subjects in this study, the questionnaire was administered to a sample of 138 first-year university students for normative comparisons. Responses for each question were compared between the two samples, and the results showed that 28 of the 30 questions differentiated significantly ($p < .05$) between students and offenders. The means and standard deviations for the full scale were 15.3 (6.0) for offenders and 22.1 (5.0) for students ($p < .001$). Internal reliability was assessed using Cronbach's coefficient α, the value of which was .87 for the two samples combined. A factor analysis showed a large first factor that appeared to measure planning and organization, and then two or three smaller factors related to boredom and concerns with present or future time.

Socialization with criminal associates outside of prison has frequently been linked with habitual offending. Therefore, we included a series of 16 questions asking about preferred modes of socialization. For each, there were three alternative answers. The middle category was considered to be characteristic of noncriminal interactions. Answers indicating frequent contacts with other offenders or an extended network of casual socialization were scored positively on the Criminal Socialization Scale. Answers at the other extreme on each question were counted on a Social Isolation Scale. Thus, each of the two scales could vary from 0 to 16, except that their sum could not exceed 16.

In preliminary analyses, it appeared that internal consistency across all items was inadequate, so some were dropped from each of the scales. Scores that will be reported are based on nine items for the Social Isolation Scale and seven for the Criminal Socialization Scale. Using these items, α was .70 and .54 for the two scales respectively. Although these values are low, especially that for the Criminal Socialization Scale, they were used as summaries of their respective sorts of specific behaviors in the absence of any better measures of the kind. It should also be noted that the items retained for the two scales were not the same selections from the original set, so they are somewhat more independent than was originally intended.

Finally, as a check on self-report and self-presentation biases, we chose the Social Desirability Scale from the Brief Personality Inventory (Jackson, 1989). This is a relatively short (16-item) scale, simply written, in language that seemed to minimize problems of administration to subjects with limited reading skills.

Several other questionnaires had been considered for inclusion but were dropped because of insufficient time for administration. Our package was designed to be completed within an hour in a single sitting, because preliminary development work had shown that additional scales led to subject fatigue or extended the time to completion considerably.

Subjects were given the questionnaires to fill out on their own, while the interviewer remained in the room. If the subject admitted to limited literacy or illiteracy, the interviewer read the material aloud to him and recorded the answers. If there was no prior indication or admission of deficient reading skills but he appeared to be taking

unusually long to go through the questions, the interviewer offered
help in reading and recording, which was usually accepted.

Occasionally there was insufficient time to finish the interview and
questionnaires before the access period was finished, and the subject
was called back for a second period. Alternatively, he was allowed to
take the questionnaires back to his cell, with the understanding that
he would return the completed forms via the institutional mail. In a
few cases, the subject was moved to a new institution before being
recalled; we attempted to arrange access in the receiving institution,
but this was not always possible, so their questionnaires were never
completed. Three subjects refused to fill out the forms, on the
grounds that they "had already done these things." (A variety of tests
were administered as part of the classification process.) Given the
numbers in the entire sample, missing data were not considered a
serious problem.

The final source of data was institutional files. Because we were
dealing with subjects soon after arrival, the availability of extensive file
information was uncertain. Entries for such areas as behavior before
arrest, or even for the current offence, were sporadic. Therefore, the
only data taken from files were on previous criminal history and basic
personal information such as age.

Data Processing

As already discussed, many of the interview questions required quan-
tified answers. In some other cases, the data were scored into discrete
categories, usually by research assistants, although when scoring or
classification required some training or experience they were done by
one of the primary investigators. Questionnaire data were scored
according to published protocols.

All data were entered into the SPSS-PC package for analyses. Distributions were checked for skew and kurtosis, and, when these exceeded reasonable limits, the raw data were subjected to logarithmic
transformation and normality rechecked before parametric inferential analyses. However, the descriptive statistics reported are all based
on untransformed data.

As described earlier, some of the original variables were deliberately redundant; in these cases correlations between the redundant

Table 2.2. *Information used in the study*

Personal history
    Age
    Highest grade completed in school (and school problems)
    Stability – longest time: in same residence, held same job, sexual relation-
        ship
    Family members with criminal history
    History of psychological problems
    Suicide attempts or ideation
    LSI (total and subscales)

Criminal history
    Total prior offences
    Total violent prior offences
    Age when first in trouble with the law
    Security level of last release

Lifestyle
    Employment
    Marital status
    Main source of income
    Criminal Socialization Scale
    Social Isolation Scale
    Time spent in various activities: family, hobbies, listening to music, TV,
        physical activity, casual socializing
    Time Use/Time Framing Scale

Release supervision
    Under supervision?
    Relationship with parole officer
    Violation of release conditions

Substance abuse
    Frequency of drug use (days/month)
    Choice and number of drugs used
    Frequency and quantity of alcohol use
    Usual effects of alcohol use: increases violence?
    Drinks and other drugs in 24 hours preoffence
    Alcohol Dependency Scale
    Drug Abuse Screening Test

Problems experienced and coping
    Specific problems at first inquiry, at later inquiry, and on timeline
    Problem seriousness ratings
    Coping Situations Questionnaire
    Relationship between problems and feelings

Table 2.2 *(cont.)*

Emotions
    Emotions in 30 days preoffence
    Emotions in 48 hours preoffence
    Emotions specified on timeline
    Beck Depression Inventory
    State Anxiety Inventory
    Multimodal Anger Inventory

Cognitions
    Rating of quality of life in preoffence period
    Confidence of success
    Thoughts specified on timeline
    Social Desirability Scale

Current offence and precursors
    Type of new offence and sentence
    Time out before revocation/rearrest
    Events specified on timeline
    Anticipatory thoughts: first passing thought to point of no return
    Responses to anticipatory thoughts
    Rehearsal and planning of offence

---

measures were calculated and proved to be very high (mostly higher than .90), so the results of only one of any such set of measures will be reported. A few other variables proved either impossible to categorize or had little variance and were discarded.

Table 2.2 is comprised of a list of the types of information included in the final data set. To facilitate statistical analysis, some of these measures were divided into several variables, and in other cases they were combined into derived variables. Therefore, the measures described in results we report will in some cases differ from those in the table.

CHAPTER THREE

Recidivists: A General Profile

Overview

This chapter presents a general description of all 311 recidivist subjects in the preoffence period. The full significance of these results can only be appreciated if the data are seen in the context of base rates, so the next chapter compares recidivists with our control group of non-recidivists. The subsequent two chapters are concerned with comparisons within the overall grouping of recidivists: Chapter 5 shows differences within the set of recidivists according to the type of current offence, that is, across the three groups in the study's design; Chapter 6 presents some further analyses of interest, such as comparisons within offence subgroups.

Personal History

We will first consider historical data for the recidivist sample, then look at behavior in the preoffence period, and finally consider precursors and the offence itself.

Examination of measures of personal background shows about what one would expect for a group of chronic serious criminal offenders; values are generally quite similar to other samples of serious offenders, especially those in the Canadian system. Means for selected measures can be seen in Table 3.1. In general, reoffenders had led

Table 3.1. *Personal and criminal history measures*

Measure	Mean (s.d.) or percent
Age	29.5 (6.8)
Highest school grade	9.5 (2.0)
Had problems at school	44.7%
Family members have criminal history	51.0%
Longest time lived in same place (mos)	27.2 (36.5)
Never more than 6 months	25.8%
Longest time held same job (mos)	26.4 (38.3)
Never more than 6 months	31.3%
Longest heterosexual relationship (mos)	37.2 (41.2)
Never more than 6 months	25.2%
Ever had any psychological problems	61.2%
Ever treated on outside	38.6%
Saw psychologist in prison	39.0%
Ever had substance abuse problem	80.0%
Ever treated for substance abuse	52.6%
Total prior convictions	25.0 (22.3)
Number of violent prior offences	3.5 (5.6)
Have no violent offences	32.2%
Age at first trouble with the law	14.6 (5.0)
First in trouble age less than 18	82.9%
LSI (max 50)	28.2 (7.6)
Current aggregate term (mos)	45.5
Time out before revocation/reconviction	7.5 (9.4)
6 months or shorter	63.2%
1 year or shorter	83.1%

unsettled lives, with frequent moves, frequent unemployment, and unstable relationships. There was, however, considerable variance in measures of previous stability, with only about one-quarter to one-third showing extreme instability.

As one would expect, subjects came from relatively poor socio-economic backgrounds, although we did not inquire about this in detail. In addition, about half said that some other family members had criminal records. We also inquired about a history of psychological problems in seven categories, from depression to psychosis, that might lead to treatment. As can be seen, the majority reported having had at least one of these problems, and almost two in five reported having received some form of professional treatment, either in prison or in the community.

The other type of problem behavior most frequent among offenders is substance abuse. On inquiry, 80% reported having had a problem with alcohol or drugs (or both) at some time in their lives, and the majority had at some time been treated for such a problem. For additional detail, we asked those who admitted to a problem about deleterious effects of substance abuse in their past, in seven different areas from finances to interpersonal relations. The mean number of areas where they said substance abuse had interfered with their lives was 3.2, with only 13% saying they had experienced no interference.

Thus, there was evidence of substantial maladaptation in subjects' lives, in addition to their criminal behavior. Many had themselves seen their problems as quite serious. Just over 25% said that they had seriously considered suicide, and 20% said that they had at some time actually attempted to kill themselves.

As would be expected given our objectives and our selection procedures, most subjects had lengthy criminal histories, as was visible in their official records and as shown in Table 3.1. The great majority had started quite young and had some history of both violent and nonviolent convictions.

Ninety-five percent had been released from their previous terms from penitentiaries, and the others from jails or provincial prisons. The majority (53.4%) had been last released from medium-security institutions, and about one-third (31.5%) from minimum-security prisons.

Once released, most had returned to prison in short order, with close to two-thirds rearrested within six months of their previous release. Even this may be an underestimate of the speed of reoffending. The numbers in the table are calculated from the elapsed time between the dates of the previous release and the new conviction or revocation of the earlier release, whichever came first. However, even if we neglect the time between offending and detection, there was usually some delay in the system. The return for a new prison term was often not a rapid process, for example, some offenders had been held several weeks – or longer – while revocation was in process, and there were often other delays such as time awaiting trial. These reasons account for the inconsistency between our recruitment criterion of reoffence within a year of release and the data shown in the table – that is, some offenders had committed new offences or had even been returned to prison after rearrest or temporary suspension of conditional release, well before their official date of reconviction or permanent revocation.

Lifestyle in the Community

In general, we conclude that we were successful in obtaining a sample of persistent serious offenders with histories that are like those described by researchers many times previously. A number of measures allow us to construct an overview of subjects' lives in the community before reoffending. The picture that results is consistent with subjects' personal histories, and again it is quite similar to other comparable populations. This information is summarized in Table 3.2.

Although subjects were asked to describe their lives in the six months before their new offences, the actual period included was often smaller because of the short total time for many between release and rearrest. If subjects' answers seem to show transitional and impermanent lifestyles, it is probably an accurate depiction. Most were living in temporary accommodations, with only a minority living in any group describable as a family. Only about one-third were married, even when common-law relationships were included.

More than half were unemployed, and many of those listed as employed were working only part time. About as many relied on unemployment insurance or welfare benefits for living expenses as on earnings from employment.

During the interview, subjects were asked to estimate how much time they spent in a variety of categories. The total time specified in all categories was summed, and the proportion of time within each category was calculated as a percentage of the total. (These categories were not designed to be unidimensional or even mutually exclusive, and it is possible for some activities to count in several categories at the same time. For example, one could watch TV with one's family. However, the figures are useful as indicators of the relative importance of

Table 3.2. *Outside lifestyle measures*

Measure	Mean (s.d.) or percent
Living in nuclear family	28.4%
Marital status:	
Currently married (including common-law)	35.1%
Single	46.3%
Other (separated, homosexual, unknown, etc.)	18.7%
Currently working (including part time)	42.1%
Principal source of income:	
Employment	34.1%
Government benefits	32.6%
Illegal activity	22.3%
Other (family, friends, etc.)	11.0%
Time use – mean proportion of time specified in:	
Family activities	12.4%
Hobbies	5.2%
Listening to music	25.3%
Watching TV	16.1%
Physical activity	9.2%
"Hanging out"	19.5%
Criminal Socialization Subscale (max = 7)	1.9 (1.6)
Social Isolation Subscale (max = 9)	2.4 (2.0)
Time Use and Time Framing Scale (max = 30)	14.6 (6.1)
Worried life not going the way you wanted?	79.0%
Rate life (1–100)	44.6 (26.2)
Mean confidence about success on outside (1–5)	2.3 (1.4)

different sorts of activities in subjects' lives.) As can be seen in Table 3.2, the largest amount of time was spent in casual or passive activities such as listening to music or "hanging out."

Given the relative lack of organized activities, one might expect that boredom would be a problem. However, this does not appear to have been the case overall. Subjects were asked to rate the frequency of boredom on a five-point scale, from "never" (assigned a value of 1) to "all the time" (rated as 5). The results were in the middle, with a mean of 2.8 (s.d. = 1.5), that is, "sometimes."

In addition to indications of instability, there are many indications that respondents were not content with their lives. Almost four in five said that they had worried that their lives were not going the way they wanted. When we asked them to rate their lives on a scale from 1 to 100, where 1 was "unbearable" and 100 was "all I'd ever want from life," 69.3% chose ratings of no more than 50.

In summary, these first data indicate that subjects' lives during their release were far from the busy, meaningful, and fruitful patterns to which most of us aspire. These are but the first intimations of the difficulties that they were experiencing. As we shall see, the rest of the information we obtained will substantiate and elaborate this first impression.

Problems and Coping

While the men in this study were on the outside they were subject to the usual range of stressors and problems. Although they clearly had substantial histories of past problems, we expected that their current problems would be more closely implicated than their histories in the immediate precipitants of offending, so we attempted to survey problems in some detail. During the interview, we asked a series of questions, from very general to quite specific, about problems experienced in the preoffence period. Later, subjects were asked to locate significant problems that had preceded the offence, on the visual timeline.

Table 3.3 summarizes the results of the problem survey, beginning with the first, open-ended inquiry. Only 12.3% of subjects said that they had experienced no problems at all, and most of the responses to the initial questions can be classified into a small set of categories. The most common problems were interpersonal conflicts (largely conflicts with heterosexual partners) and substance abuse, with financial problems ranked third.

A total of 17 possible problem areas were surveyed in the specific inquiries. The categories were chosen on the basis of past experience with problems mentioned by inmates in similar research, and from clinical experience. Most inmates admitted to having experienced several problems on the list, with only 3.0% (still) denying any at all, and 12.9% specifying only one problem area.

Results from particular problem categories generally confirm the

Table 3.3. *Problems experienced after release*

Measure	Mean (s.d.) or percent
Problems mentioned at first inquiry:	
Interpersonal conflict	25.2%
Substance abuse	21.3%
Money/financial	18.1%
Work/school	11.9%
None at all	12.3%
Total number mentioned after listing and search (possible 17)	3.6 (1.8)
Mentioned on timeline:	
Interpersonal	38.4%
Female relationships[a]	27.9%
Friends[a]	10.7%
Parents[a]	4.5%
Siblings[a]	2.3%
Substance (ab)use	33.4%
Money	23.7%
(Un)employment	20.5%
Parole or supervision	7.1%
Feelings/moods	8.1%
Problem seriousness ratings (0–10):	
Substance abuse	5.4 (4.3)
Money/financial	4.9 (4.0)
Work/school/unemployment	4.4 (4.1)
Physical or emotional health	3.9 (3.6)
Wife or family	3.5 (3.8)
Release supervision	3.5 (3.9)
Housing or living situation	2.7 (3.5)
Friends	2.6 (3.2)
Time (boredom, activities available, etc.)	2.6 (3.2)

[a] Subcategories do not add to total figure for family/friends because of overlap.

impression from the open-ended inquiry. As expected, just over 80% of subjects said that they had a substance abuse problem, and roughly the same number had been experiencing conflict or difficulties in at least one interpersonal relationship. About half had experienced difficulties with money or finances. Problems related to unemployment were also frequent, cited by almost half of the sample, while only about 8% mentioned difficulties in their work situation, not surprising given the low rate of employment.

These frequency data must be evaluated cautiously, because they might be influenced by the list of specific problems surveyed. Nevertheless, the similarities to the results of the first inquiry are substantial, despite the differences in the methods.

Additional confirmation comes from the timeline data, as summarized in the middle of Table 3.3. These data were gathered at the end of the interview, after the problem survey had covered a variety of possible problem areas, so a specification of any problem at this point was not likely to have been influenced by its ease of recall or recency, as might have been the case in the first inquiry.

Our final source of information does yield a slightly different ordering than the other methods. Near the end of the interview, subjects were given a set of nine categories, from substance abuse and lack of money to difficulties in the use of their time. (Our experience had been that the latter was never mentioned spontaneously by prisoners, although it is sometimes seen as a problem by nonoffenders in the community, so it was included as a control for situational demands.) They were asked to rate the seriousness of any problems they might have experienced in each category, on a 10-point scale.

The percentages of subjects who rated problems in the various categories as more than minimal, that is, higher than 1 out of 10, were quite similar to the rates of mention with the other measures. However, the mean-rated seriousness, as shown at the bottom of Table 3.3, was highest for substance abuse, followed by money and (un)employment problems, whereas interpersonal conflicts (wife or family) were ranked only in the middle of the set. Thus, although interpersonal problems were the most common, sometimes when they occurred they were not seen as very serious.

The most important result here is that the problems subjects perceived in their lives outside of prison are largely from a relatively small set of categories that far outrank all others. These problems are neither esoteric nor unusual; rather, such things as interpersonal conflict are common, even pervasive, in contemporary life, and few of us are fortunate enough never to have felt that we were facing straitened finances. The exact ordering of categories is not critical, for it is the average of a group of individuals, and what mattered for each subject was his unique individual set of problems.

Our theoretical model assumes that problems occur for offenders as for anyone else, but that their ineffective ways of responding to problems is one of the important areas that distinguishes repeat offenders from other individuals. It has been clearly shown previously (Zamble and Porporino, 1988) that convicted offenders typically have poor coping ability. However, given the important theoretical function of coping, we had included a measure of it among the questionnaires. The standardized coping inventory asked subjects to describe how they would have handled each of a set of five problem situations. Responses to each situation were rated according to likely effectiveness and also for exacerbation of the problem (Zamble and Porporino, 1988).

In general, the tactics shown in subjects' responses were a head-on attack on the problem, aimed at alleviating it for the moment. Typically there was no evidence of any analysis of the problem situation or weighing of possible alternatives, nor did there appear to have been much anticipation of the consequences of the first responses. This was very consistent with previous accounts of offenders' coping behavior.

On a functional 16-point scale, with assignable scores from 4 to 20, there was little difference in the mean efficacy ratings across the five situations, with a range from 9.9 to 10.7 (and s.d.'s from 2.2 to 2.8). Overall, 66.0% of subjects would have adopted a response to at least one situation that would likely make the situation worse. These results are comparable to previous results for imprisoned offenders and quite different from the assessed levels of coping efficacy for a nonoffender population (Hughes and Zamble, 1993).

While this apparently poor quality of coping replicated previous results, the self-efficacy data from the same questionnaire showed that subjects were not aware of the limitations of their ways of coping. The mean self-rating of efficacy was 5.2 (s.d. = 1.2) on a seven-point scale, a level showing some (misplaced) self-confidence by subjects in their coping abilities. This inaccuracy may help to explain why offenders persist in their often disastrous ways of coping with common problematic situations.

Supervision

A distinctive feature of subjects' lives was supervision by parole authorities, a fact of life for three-quarters of them at the time of their new offences. This monitoring and control by authorities was one way in which their experiences differed from those of most people living in the open community. Examination of the role of supervision in their lives and its effect on their behavior can provide some instructive information for the correctional system, as well as further information on subjects' experiences.

In itself, being supervised seems to have had very little effect. Only about one-third (33.8%) said that their release terms presented any difficulties, but the primary reason for this was probably that the restrictions imposed in their release terms were commonly and quickly ignored. The majority (55.6%) reported that they had broken their release terms in the first week.

The figures for some specific types of violations strengthen the impression about the ineffectiveness of supervision. Over two-thirds of subjects had had restrictions on the use of alcohol or drugs. Nevertheless, 72.4% of those with restrictions (and 78.3% of the total sample) reported that they had used alcohol in the first week of their release, and 61.4% had used at least one illegal drug in the first week.

Both absolutely and relatively, the prohibitions imposed under supervision did not limit substance abuse. In fact, in some ways they may even have hindered efforts at control. Although we did not ask about it specifically, several subjects mentioned that they had wanted to enter community substance abuse programs but had been unable to do so because they would first have had to admit to a current problem, an admission that would have led to revocation of their release. Admissions of problems in self-control were impossible under the system, but violations were easy.

The lack of effectiveness cannot be attributed to personal difficulties with parole officers. Most subjects indicated that they had gotten along reasonably well with their parole officers: On a five-point scale, the mean was 2.5, halfway between "well" and "satisfactorily." Neither did subjects feel that their supervisors had failed them in some easily specifiable way. Half could think of nothing the parole officer could have done differently within the system that would have helped. ("He just did his job. It didn't hurt me, it didn't help.") Only 18.9% said that the parole officer had hindered them on the outside, and 35.1% said that he or she had helped, so the net effect was seen by subjects as positive, but generally trivial. Given the data on violations, we would agree.

Emotions

Given the occurrence of a variety of problems and inadequate coping resources to deal with them, one would expect some negative emotional consequences. From our analogy of recidivism to a relapse process, we would also expect that dysphoric emotional states would have been especially common before the new offence.

Therefore, we used a variety of measures of subjects' feelings in the preoffence period. The various measures were intended to show different aspects of emotional states, for example, they referenced different time periods, but, consonant with our interview strategy, they were also somewhat redundant in order to provide mutual confirmation.

First are the results of several standardized questionnaires that asked subjects to report their emotional states from the final month preceding their new offence. Summary statistics are shown in the bottom section of Table 3.4.

From these it would appear that depression and anxiety were very serious problems for many subjects in the period. Two-thirds of the sample had scores on the Beck Depression Inventory indicating some possibility of at least a mild longer-term depressive state (10 or higher), over 40% scored at least at the level of moderate (19 or higher) depression, and 15% reached the "severe" category. Similarly, the majority had scores on the State Anxiety Inventory above the mean for a standardization sample of patients diagnosed with anxiety reactions. Although we do not have clinical comparison levels for the anger measures, they are quite high in comparison to previously reported levels for normal populations.

One must be cautious in interpreting these scores because of their

Table 3.4. *Emotions in preoffence period*

Emotional state	Measure (percentages)				
	Strong (30 days)	Strong (48 hours)	Time-line	Strongest (30 days)	Strongest (48 hours)
Hopelessness	17.5	12.3	7.5	3.2	4.3
Depression	38.2	24.3	28.9	18.5	11.8
Moody/brooding	18.1	12.3	4.9	2.9	2.3
Anger	31.1	27.5	32.8	10.1	15.8
Frustration	39.8	30.7	19.8	11.7	10.9
Stressed	27.5	19.7	13.3	7.1	5.6
Anxiety	35.6	23.9	21.4	13.6	10.9
Guilt	15.9	7.4	4.9	3.2	1.6
Loneliness	22.7	14.6	8.8	4.5	2.0
Bored	23.6	11.4	8.8	2.6	1.3
Sexual frustration	5.2	3.9	0.6	0.6	0.7
Nothing/numb	11.7	10.7	2.6	1.9	5.3
Positive (all)	35.6	29.8	41.2	17.9	21.4
Other	9.5	10.4	14.0	1.9	6.3
Any dysphoric[a]	79.7	67.8	76.5	77.2	65.0
Major dysphoric[b]	62.7	52.7	61.4	42.1	37.5

Questionnaire measures (mean and s.d. or percentage)

Beck Depression Inventory	17.0 (12.2)
Moderate or severe (19 or higher)	40.4%
State Anxiety Inventory	48.6 (13.3)
Scores 46 or higher	56.1%
Multimodal Anger Inventory Subscales:	
Anger Arousal	17.5 (7.3)
Anger Expression	22.5 (6.6)
Hostility	11.6 (13.8)
Anger In	13.2 (5.4)
Anger Out	6.1 (1.6)

[a] One or more of the first 10 listed states, from hopelessness to boredom.
[b] One or more of depression, anger, or anxiety.

retrospective nature. Although subjects were instructed to answer in terms of their feelings in the preoffence period, many of the questions call for very specific information that may be difficult to divorce from the present, and the results may have been influenced by subjects' moods at the time of testing, even more than other questions about emotions and feelings. Nevertheless, they do show levels of depression and anxiety that are even higher than the substantial distress measured previously among prisoners at the beginning of their terms (Zamble and Porporino, 1988). Thus, our first indications are of serious emotional maladjustment during the period of interest.

Confirmation is provided by other measures. An important section of the interview asked subjects to describe their emotional state in the month preceding the offence. Although the process began with an open-ended inquiry, it led up to the presentation of a list of 14 emotional states from "hopelessness" to "other" (not classifiable in any other category), from which we compiled a list of all of the strong emotions/feelings that each subject had experienced during the period. The process was then repeated for a shorter time period, namely, the 48 hours preceding the offence. If a subject had listed several different states during either period, as was usually the case, we also asked him to specify the single strongest emotional state during the respective period. Finally, as for problems and thoughts, at the end of the interview respondents were asked to locate their emotions on a preoffence timeline.

These measures each show very similar results, as may be seen in Table 3.4. Frustration, depression, anxiety, and anger were all common in the month before the offence, each reported by about one-third of subjects. Feelings of stress and boredom were also common, along with loneliness, each reported by about one-quarter of the sample.

To get a summary measure of emotional dysphoria, we combined the first 10 categories, that is, all except sexual frustration, lack of any feelings, and positive states, and the result showed that four out of five subjects had experienced some strong negative emotional state in the period covered. If we combine only the triad of most common clinical dysphoric states – depression, anxiety, and anger – a substantial majority of subjects are still included. In contrast, only half as many reported any strong positive feelings during the same period.

When we compare these results to those for only the very end of the preoffence period, we would expect all frequencies to be lower in the shorter period, and this is the case, with most values about one-third lower. At the same time, the relative ordering is mostly the same. Among the dysphoric emotions, anger and frustration (two related states) appear to be exceptions because they decrease proportionately less. Anger moves from being the fourth most common negative state to second in the final 48 hours, while frustration remains the most frequently cited. Thus, in the longer period subjects seem to have been generally unhappy, with high but roughly equal rates of occurrence of a variety of negative emotional states. As the offence became imminent, the diffusely negative moods channeled increasingly into frustration and anger.

Data from the timeline provide more confirmation, and also some elucidation of changes over time. Many subjects said that they had begun the period very positively, usually just following their release from prison, so a greater proportion listed some positive feelings on the timeline than with the oral listing method. ("I was really happy to be out." "Everything looked terrific.") Later, their moods had darkened. Anger was the most frequently specified negative state overall on the timeline, and this was especially evident for the last several days preceding the offence. ("I was pissed off at everything and everybody.")

A person may experience a variety of emotions over time, and one might see something like the above results for almost any group of people, although normally with less preponderance of negative states over positive. We can characterize subjects' overall states better (or to see better the link to extreme or unusual actions) by considering which emotions predominated in the mix of feelings. Figures on the right side of Table 3.4 show what subjects chose as their single strongest state for each of the two measurement periods.

As may be seen, these measures sharpen the apparent importance of depression, anger, frustration, and anxiety. For both periods, these four together account for over half of the total and add up to roughly three times the figure for positive feelings. In contrast, the importance of other categories decrease disproportionately from the listings of all emotions experienced. Although such feelings occurred fairly frequently, they rarely predominated in subjects' moods. Comparing the strongest single emotion for the different time periods, we can again see a shift toward a predominant mood of anger as the offence approached, even more clearly than in the frequencies for all strong emotions.

As a final source of information on emotional states, we asked subjects what they thought had set off their feelings in the preoffence period, and they had little difficulty in answering. Most saw their emotional states as having been consequences of particular problems. Interpersonal relationships (37.4%) were the most frequently implicated, and substance abuse (26.8%) and money problems (23.5%) were also common.

However, the second most common attribution (29.7%) was to internal dispositions for certain feelings rather than as a response to specific conditions or situations. Very few saw their emotional states as being related to a psychological problem, or to some dysfunction. Rather, they saw their reactions as generalized and unrelated to specific events, for example, "That was just the way I was feeling; it was all inside of me."

Thus, the majority of subjects did perceive connections between their feelings and events in their environment at the time, although they had not been successful in controlling those events by their actions. However, for a substantial minority strong emotional states were "free-floating" and not seen as tied to specific events. This reflects either some psychogenic origins, which even the subjects themselves seemed to think quite unlikely, or (again) a considerable lack of self-awareness and insight.

Thoughts

In addition to problems and emotions, we asked subjects to describe their thoughts in the preoffence period, again using the visual aid of the timeline. Our original intention had been to assess the sequential relationships between cognitions, emotions, and problematic events in parallel timelines for the same period. However, this task proved exceedingly difficult. There was much imprecision about the timing, and subjects were not usually able to give exact information about the sequences of events, emotions, and thoughts. At best, one could judge that certain sets were roughly contemporaneous.

Sometimes a particular type of thought was specified as occurring continuously over the entire 30-day period covered. There were also large blank segments on at least the thoughts timeline for about one-quarter of the subjects. Moreover, there was confusion between the lines for events and thoughts. Items recorded on the timeline for emotions were generally recognizable as emotions or feelings, but the lines specified for either thoughts or events often included the other (e.g., "I was working, nothing else" was on the thoughts line, but "I knew I was going to be fired" was written on the events line).

Although it made the identification of sequential relationships impossible, this seems reasonable: When a person is engaged for significant periods of time in a major event or activity, his or her thoughts may be largely or even entirely concerned with that event or activity. Therefore, our categories for classifying thoughts included several that described common events, to capture what was occupying subjects' attention, rather than more strictly including only cognitions.

The final set of categories and their frequencies of mention are shown in Table 3.5. Predictably, the most frequently recorded types of thoughts are those related to mundane life events, such as interactions with family and friends or employment. The importance of such categories mirrors their appearance in the lists of problems in the same period. If subjects perceived problems in certain areas, it is not surprising that their thoughts were concerned with those same areas. Concerns with parole, police, or other authorities were also frequently seen in the set of responses, more so than in the list of common problems.

Other categories are not so reflective of external events. Among these, the most frequent category was comprised of optimistic or positive thoughts about the present or the future ("I'm happy to be out [of prison]; I can really make it this time"). For many subjects, there were also thoughts about self-improvement or change that might realistically have helped them to adapt on the outside ("Next month I will go back to school"), although there was unfortunately much more thought than action in this vein. On the other hand, these were balanced by almost as many diffuse negative cognitions and defeatist (though likely realistic) thoughts about the inevitability of return to

Table 3.5. *Thoughts in preoffence period (from timeline)*

Category	Percentage mentioned
Interpersonal	48.0
Money	23.7
Substance (ab)use	31.5
Employment	35.4
Parole/authorities	18.3
General negative conditions	11.4
Criminal – instrumental	11.7
Criminal – emotive	5.5
Return to prison	10.1
Reform/self-improvement	11.0
Positive/optimistic	16.6

prison. One could also see descriptions of thoughts about the resumption of criminal activity, sometimes for instrumental purposes and sometimes to satisfy emotional needs such as revenge, but almost always as a perceived way of dealing with a particular problem. ("Money's almost gone [buying drugs]; I'll go in with [a friend], doing robberies to raise money.")

To assess changes over time, thoughts in each category were counted separately as they appeared at either the first or second half of the preoffence period. There were no major trends among the categories dealing with specific events or problems, except that thoughts about employment were much less visible at the end of the period than at the beginning.

However, there were changes in frequencies for nonspecific cognitions. Optimistic and reform-minded entries were about half as frequent just before the offence as earlier, but concerns about return to prison doubled, and global negative thoughts increased by about a factor of five. Of course, thoughts about the commission of criminal activities also rose, although only a small minority of subjects mentioned having such thoughts even at the very end of the period. Apparently, few subjects were involved in planning or preparation for their imminent offences, a point we shall elaborate on later.

General Changes

In general, it appeared that for many subjects a generally positive pattern of thoughts had deteriorated into pessimism in the period before the commission of new offences. As a measure of such changes, we inspected all three of the timelines together, that is, those for events, emotions, and thoughts, and characterized the general trend over the 30-day period. Downward trends were visible in about one-quarter of the charts, as compared to very few (2%) with more positive outlooks closer to the offence. Almost half were consistently negative over the period, and only the remaining 27% were judged to show a consistently positive or even neutral level. Thus, the outlook of the substantial majority of recidivists was negative before the offence, and for many of these men there had been a visible change in cognitions or mood over the final month.

The change was particularly visible for those who had been released within the 30-day period of the timeline. By their own admission, 21.3% of the entire sample had been on the street less than a month before the (first) new offence (not including technical violations of release terms or minor infractions). This figure should be compared to the 8.1% who were rearrested in the same period: The arm of the law may be long, but it is not quick. For most of these subjects, events on the timeline illustrated a very quick decline from the relief and optimism at the time of release as it turned into defeat, anger, or hopelessness.

However, downward trends were not visible for all of the short-latency reoffenders. Some had crime-free periods too short to characterize, because their new offences were within a few days of their release, as if they had been on a ballistic course waiting to impact. (The shortest period was undoubtedly for the man who robbed the taxi driver taking him from the prison to the train station; he was rearrested before the train left.)

If such deteriorative trends did occur, it is important to know whether they were accompanied or preceded by events that might have acted as triggers. This is critical for the possibility of monitoring releasees to track the critical events, in order to direct assistance and intervention to the points of need. We counted two different categories of events on the timelines for all subjects. The first count includes things that would be listed on a survey of negative significant life events, such as a death in the family or ending a relationship or a job. For example, one subject had survived well for about a year, when his wife was diagnosed with cancer; within three months he was back in prison. Twenty-two percent of the time lines had such events apparent in the month or so preceding the new offence.

One's moods or thoughts are also affected by many events that are not changes in the course of one's life. For example, a conflict with a spouse would not be included on a scale of life events unless it ends the relationship, but it certainly does have a temporary effect, and both the conflict itself and its sequelae present challenges to one's coping ability. Therefore, the second count of special events on the timeline looked for evidence of significant problems requiring the exercise of coping skills. ("I knew I was probably going to lose my job." "My girlfriend said she wanted to move out [but she did not go].") In addition to specific situations, we also included evidence of general failures to cope, that is, "gave up."

Just under half of the timeline sheets appeared to show such coping challenges, with about 22% interpersonal problems and 25% other sorts. In contrast, about 17% of the timelines showed confused or unclear events or had very little material to judge, and another 9% contained explicit denials of problems. Another substantial number (23%) showed clear evidence of steady substance abuse for at least part of the period.

We would certainly not argue that this classification is rigorous, because the categories are neither rigorously defined nor mutually exclusive, and we have no information on the reliability of the scoring. (Development and validation of improved classification schemes are tasks for the future.) However, they do provide additional evidence that many subjects were faced with events that must have taxed or exceeded their coping resources. If one combines these men with those who show major involvement with substance abuse, it is evident that maladaptive patterns were present before the offence for the great majority of the recidivist sample.

Difficult situations in themselves do not ordinarily lead to disastrous results; rather, for most people they are *challenges* to coping resources. However, given the evidence already presented about the poor coping ability of our subjects, we would expect problematic situations to lead to deterioration in emotional states and changes in the character of thoughts. Therefore, we looked at the relationships between the special events counted on the timelines, both significant life events and coping challenges, and the patterns of changes over time in thoughts and emotions described earlier.

Among subjects for whom a negative life event was visible, about 40% showed a deteriorating mood pattern, with 51% uniformly negative and only 9% positive or level. By comparison, among those without any significant life events visible only 15% had downward mood trends, and 47% were uniformly negative, but 38% were positive, level, or improving. (Although release from prison might be considered a major life event, subjects who were released during the 30-day reference period were omitted from these comparisons.) Statistically, there is strong evidence of an association between life events and deteriorating moods ($X^2(2) = 27.30$, $p < .001$).

Similarly, subjects with coping challenges indicated on their timelines were also more likely to show undesirable changes in emotions and thoughts. About 71% of those with no clear indications of difficult situations had level, positive, or improving moods, as compared to only 14% of those with visible coping challenges. At the other end of the continuum, 31% of those with coping challenges showed increasingly negative moods and cognitions (and 55% were consistently negative), whereas only 5% of those with no apparent problem were falling (and 24% consistently negative). Again, the association is statistically quite strong ($X^2(2) = 73.10$, $p < .001$).

These results are challengeable on the grounds that all of the ratings were done from the same sets of material, so they may have been confounded. The ratings were done at different times, and an attempt was made to code life events and coping challenges independently of the rest of the material on the sheets, but we cannot say with complete confidence that this was accomplished successfully. However, the magnitude of the associations is, at the very least, strongly suggestive. In addition, we will present later some (limited) evidence that the rated patterns of mood changes have predictive value, which would presuppose some minimum level of reliability.

Of course, even if the ratings are entirely reliable, there is no assurance that even a completely informed observer on the spot would have been able to predict the imminence of a new offence. The judgments made here were with the benefit of hindsight, and in particular with the ability to specify the reference point of a new offence. However, the present results do indicate that new offences do not occur in a psychological vacuum, but rather that in many cases there are identifiable stress points before the initiation of an offence sequence.

If we conclude as detached observers that events likely to increase the possibility of a relapse sequence were happening in offenders' lives, one wonders about subjects' own perceptions of determinative events. When we asked them whether they thought that difficulties they had been experiencing in the period were related to their new offences, 82.1% said yes. Given the (deliberately) loose wording of this question, this can be regarded as an upper bound on the proportion of subjects who perceived a relationship between events and offences.

In an attempt to get a more detailed answer, we asked them to tell us what they thought had led to the offence. Most of the answers could be classified into a relatively small number of groups, as shown in Table 3.6. For the sample as a whole, the largest single number of categorized answers was the need or desire for money. However, two categories indicated an emotional basis, a category of specific emotions (e.g., "I was angry and frustrated.") and what we characterize in the table as out of control (e.g., "I just blew up."). These combine to about the same percentage as financial motives. Some other answers that have been proposed previously as major sources of criminal motivation, such as peer instigation or pressure, were mentioned rarely if ever.

Thus, the majority of subjects did have some attributions of the proximal causes of their new criminal behaviors. However, their perceptions did not go beyond their state of mind immediately before the offence to include any more distal events. If they remembered that they had been angry, they did not consider the sources of that anger. If they recalled being motivated by a desire for money, they did not question whether their actions had constituted an optimal solution to their needs. The majority of subjects did have some self-awareness but little insight past their own rationalizations.

Moreover, our questions about awareness of the causes of new offences showed a sizeable minority of subjects who could express no explanation at all for their behavior and maintained that "things just happened" to them. This proportion was about 30% for the direct question about the causes of their offence(s). Clearly, the events that

Table 3.6. *Subjects' perceptions of what led to offence*

Category description	Percentage
Driven by emotion (mostly anger)	20.2
Out of control	10.4
Needed money	32.6
Boredom	2.0
Peer pressure	3.3
Sexual frustration	1.6
"It just happened" (no explanation)	14.7
Other, unclassifiable	15.3

led to the resumption of their criminal careers did not include much awareness or conscious choice for these subjects.

Alcohol and Drug Use

One of the distinguishing features of any account of the preoffence period for any group of offenders is usually much consumption of alcohol and drugs. This population is no exception. A variety of questions were included in the interview to get detailed data on usage, both generally while living on the outside and also immediately before the offence. We also employed standardized questionnaires to measure dependency and the accumulated ill effects of substance abuse.

As summarized in Table 3.7, the very lowest estimate of the percentage affected by substance use is the more than one-third of the sample who included it among events on the timeline. Sometimes the event mentioned was the resumption of use after a period of abstinence, but often a subject specified drug or alcohol use over the whole period, as a prominent feature of his life.

Other measures determined amounts of use for all subjects, not just those who thought it a prominent feature of their lives. During our standard reference period, that is, the six months preceding rearrest, most of the recidivists regularly used alcohol, and the majority ingested other drugs illegally. Moderation was not common, and those who did use alcohol or drugs did so with some regularity, and, on the average, in high amounts, as may be seen from the table.

Table 3.7. *Measures of alcohol*[a] *and drug use*

Measure	Mean (s.d.) or percentage
Substance abuse visible on timeline	37.3%
Mean score on Alcohol Dependency Scale	8.3 (9.8)
Mean score on Drug Abuse Screening Test	6.6 (5.4)
General preoffence period:	
Used alcohol	80.3%
Averaged at least 6 drinks daily	26.5%
Daily intake for drinkers	7.5 (11.7)
Alcohol increases violence	21.0%
Used other drugs illegally	59.2%
Used daily	29.9%
Number of different drugs for users	1.6 (0.9)
Days/month users take any drugs	19.1 (12.1)
Last day (24 hrs) before offence:	
Used any alcohol	56.0%
Consumed at least 6 drinks	42.4%
Mean alcohol intake for those drinking	18.6 (18.1)
Used any other drugs illegally	33.0%
Number of different drugs for users	1.2 (0.5)
Days in a row drugs had been used	14.0 (14.2)

[a] Results for alcohol use are converted to standard drinks, i.e., the amount of absolute alcohol in 1.5 ounces of spirits, a 12 ounce bottle of Canadian (5%) beer, or a 5 ounce glass of wine.

To see the relationship between alcohol and violence, we asked subjects to rate how frequently they were violent when drinking, on a five-point scale. The result was subtracted from their estimate of how frequently they were violent when not drinking, to give a measure of whether alcohol increased the likelihood of violent behavior. Although the difference was "0" for most subjects, representing no perceived difference, one in five had scores indicating that alcohol may have increased their propensities to violence. (As expected, none had scores indicating that alcohol decreased violent tendencies.) Analyses in a subsequent chapter will consider whether this measure may be useful in differentiating the type of new offence.

Aside from alcohol, the drugs used most commonly were cannabis (37.9% of subjects) and cocaine (29.3%). The figures for cocaine use are in line with other contemporary reports, but they are much higher than in a comparable sample of inmates in our previous research (Zamble and Porporino, 1988); a decade earlier, cocaine use had been very infrequent among offenders in Canadian penitentiaries.

Comparisons between the figures for the general period and those for the 24-hour period preceding the offence show some interesting differences. A majority reported that they had been drinking immediately before the offence, and for those the average intake was more than double the average for the longer period. At such levels, even most experienced heavy drinkers would have been intoxicated. In addition, most of the one-third of the sample who customarily used drugs other than alcohol had been through a period of continuous usage. The drug of choice here was clearly cocaine, used in the day before the offence by a reported 20.5% of all reoffenders, as compared to only 15.3% for cannabis.

In summary, along with other events in the period, there appears to have been an increase in already high levels of substance usage in the day immediately preceding the new offence. This raises the question of where substance abuse fits into the sequence of preoffence events. Unfortunately, there does not seem to be any consistent answer. From the sequence of events on the timeline, it appears that substance abuse was sometimes the final response to a particular event or problem, that is, the beginning of a coping breakdown. In other cases, the alcohol or drug use seems to have occurred first, and other difficulties – including the offence – followed as its consequences.

Offenders themselves were not much help in answering this question. We asked them to tell us what went through their minds when they thought of drinking, and the greatest number (36.8%) said that it just felt pleasant, and about as many more said that they didn't think anything because it was just a habit, or that they didn't know why.

We conclude that for the majority of offenders substance abuse is so entangled with other maladaptive behaviors that they may be inseparable. It is unlikely that there is any single relationship that applies in all cases, just as there is no single path leading to criminal offending generally. There are undoubtedly several different roles that substance abuse can play, each involved in one of the different offence paths. Some light may be shed on this question when we consider different types of current offences in Chapter 5. Whatever the eventual answer(s), for now we can say that it is as foolish to attempt to change offenders' coping problems without dealing with substance abuse as it would be to treat the substance abuse without improving their ways of dealing with problems in their environment. In any case, the use of intoxicants is certainly an important part of the antecedents of re-offending.

Factor Analysis

Given the number of variables in this study, and the variety of domains that they sample, it takes some effort to fit the pattern of results into a comprehensive picture. Expectations from our theoretical perspective may be helpful in this regard, but a more empirical technique for reducing the complexity of the dataset is also desirable, especially for readers not (or not yet) convinced of the usefulness of our model. Therefore, we performed the first of a set of multivariate analyses, in this case a factor analysis intended to reduce the number of variables to a more manageable set and to illustrate some of the natural dimensions of the variable set.

Other multivariate analyses will be included in the chapters that follow. It is not necessary for the reader to comprehend these analyses in order to follow our basic argument or to understand the basic implications of the results. However, we expect that they will enrich the understanding of readers with more advanced statistical knowledge.

For the analyses reported here, and in the following chapters, only measures of offence antecedents were considered; in effect, this means that indices of the offence process itself considered in the following section were omitted. The remaining set of variables was severely winnowed. First, measures with poor statistical properties, such as minimal variance, were eliminated. From the great majority of surviving variables, those that significantly differentiated recidivists from the nonrecidivist comparison sample (see Chapter 4) were selected, to ensure that the measures used were all specific to recidivism. Finally, correlations within this set were calculated; when pairs of related variables were correlated beyond a moderate level (above .50) one of the pair was dropped.

Table 3.8. *Factor loadings for five-factor varimax rotation solution*

Variable	Rotten life	Substance use	Dynamic dysphoria	Money reaction	Protective behaviors
Substance abuse problem	.38854	.61380	.06424	.26918	−.10147
Emotional problem	.58326	.05309	.12891	.13692	.05972
Interpersonal (family) problem	.38761	.21529	.16149	.15451	.13000
Money problem	.26735	−.02596	.01994	.54496	.01012
Supervisor problem	.34217	−.18576	.05144	−.20431	.13143
Previous psychological problems	.42228	.10282	.12410	.13678	.38471
Anger in 24 hours preoffence	.11511	.12597	.57080	−.36731	.18000
Anxiety in 24 hours preoffence	.08726	−.09350	.47341	.24261	.11223
Depression in 24 hours preoffence	.20575	.05253	.59008	.10704	.08900
Frustrated in 24 hours preoffence	.06381	−.14393	.69341	−.04868	−.01514
Positive mood in 24 hours preoffence	−.34083	−.02654	−.44385	−.24839	.19456
Beck Depression Inventory	.81291	.04274	.10455	.15534	−.06817
State Anxiety Inventory	.67438	.02590	.29101	.11886	−.04211
Anger Arousal Subscale	.58847	.97666	.12149	−.36827	−.05190
Deteriorating outlook	.26165	.02048	.47294	.35090	−.17670

Drinks in 24 hours preoffence	.1519	.64482	−.07179	−.36210	.11010
Days continuous drug use 24 hours preoffence	.10720	.25948	.08027	.37179	−.09827
Average daily drinks (FQI)	.11014	.73189	−.08441	−.19236	.02438
Number of drug types used	.15357	.40346	.29556	.32778	.01582
Time Use Scale	−.28442	−.28680	.04487	−.06839	.47992
Criminal Socialization Scale	−.04734	−.18463	−.01893	−.20764	−.64446
Social Isolation Scale	.41126	−.24717	−.13017	.02543	.57179
Social Desirability Scale	−.69084	−.08596	−.05970	.07795	.13166
Frequency bored	.43480	.03263	.07522	.26792	−.24904
Thought of negative consequences	.00526	−.03245	.19577	.46923	.10483
Percent of time "hanging out"	−.07971	.62302	−.03540	.15990	−.05004
Under suprvision	.00202	−.28987	.19823	−.24684	.27693
Employed	−.18811	.00309	.11592	−.28928	.45974
Rating of quality of life	−.60284	−.02605	−.08999	−.16258	−.00640
Coping adequacy	.56125	.20407	.07871	.40624	.21206

This yielded approximately 35 remaining measures. Given our interest in showing the role of current dynamic factors, historical measures (such as the age of first criminal offences or educational attainment) were of secondary importance, so these were also dropped from the set used for the analyses to be reported. However, most analyses were duplicated with historical measures included, and the results did not generally further elucidate or improve on those that will be shown, so they will not be reported.

The factor analyses pertaining to the material in this chapter thus included a total of 30 variables, sampling behavior and events in several areas. They included several measures of the occurrence or severity of perceived problems and a set of indices of emotional states, as well as quantifications of drug and alcohol use. Some measures of specific behaviors or cognitions in the preoffence period were also included, for example, the pattern of socialization and the amount of time spent "hanging out," time framing, whether the respondent was working and/or under supervision, and how he rated his quality of life. Finally, there were a few variables related to coping, specifically our assessment of whether the timeline showed a deterioration in (or a uniformly negative) level of emotions and cognitions, and the ratio of coping efficacy to the number of problems experienced, used as a measure of the adequacy of coping skills.

The list of variables used can be seen in Table 3.8. It should be emphasized that these are almost exclusively measures of behavior current to the preoffence period and do not include any information on previous criminal behavior or on social or economic origins. The closest any come to historical information is the measure of how many different types of psychological problems a subject had experienced in his life.

Summarized in the table is a principal components analysis with a varimax rotation. A substantial first factor emerged in the unrotated solution, accounting for approximately 19% of the variance, but after this there were nine other smaller factors with eigenvalues greater than 1. A scree plot showed an unusually smooth curve, so the choice of how many factors to use is fairly arbitrary. We looked at solutions including from 5 to 10 rotated factors, and they appeared quite similar. Factor loadings for the five-factor solution, accounting for 43% of the variance, are shown in the table.

As can be seen, the first and largest factor is fairly general, with loadings above .3 for almost half of the measures. It appears to measure a pervasive dysphoric state, with experiences of a variety of serious problems in living combined with negative moods and cognitions and a lack of concern with socially desirable responses. The next two factors are much more specific and relatively easy to understand. The second is fairly clearly related to drug and alcohol usage, while the third factor includes specific emotions in the preoffence period and the change in states over time. The remaining two factors are somewhat harder to interpret. The fourth has strongest loadings from money problems, inadequate coping, anticipation of consequences, drug (but not alcohol) use, and feelings of anger and anxiety. This may show a component of something approaching deliberate choice of a new offence for certain offenders (cf. Chapter 5). Finally, the fifth factor includes mostly measures of components of a normal noncriminal lifestyle, such as holding a job and not socializing with people involved in criminal behavior, but it also has loadings from previous psychological problems and social isolation; together, these may play a protective role.

Solutions with a greater number of rotated factors give the same sorts of information. With more factors, some of the factors in the model shown here are split into smaller factors; for instance, substance abuse is divided into alcohol and other drug use. Thus, there appears to be some support on a multivariate level for our general position that problems experienced, emotional reactions, substance use, and certain specific behaviors including coping all play important roles as antecedents of recidivism.

The Offence Process

A criminal offence does not fall from a discontinuity in the behavioral continuum, but rather it occurs as part of a sequence of behaviors. An offence often produces considerable changes in the lives of the persons involved, both offenders and, especially, victims. However, it is the occurrence of the offence that represents a breakpoint and that triggers the consequences, not the sequence of events leading up to it.

One can usually pinpoint the time at which an ordinary action sequence becomes a predatory criminal offence. Before that point, an

offence is part of a series of actions like any other. It should be subject
to the same influences as other behaviors, and it is adopted for enactment by the same control or decision mechanisms as any other course
of behavior. A person will usually have thoughts of new behaviors
before they are enacted, and there is often planning and consideration of whether and when to take that particular course of action.
Conscious decision processes are sometimes minimized, as for individuals we consider "impulsive," or for most of us if the behavior has
become habitual or automatic after past practice, but even then a set
of antecedent conditions that control the evocation of actions should
be identifiable.

Thus, in addition to gathering information about events in subjects'
lives that might work as precursors to a relapse into reoffending, we
also gathered information on events that are part of the offence
process. We were led to construct a series of anticipatory events that
we hoped would elucidate the course of offense onset.

The primary device for this was our timeline of critical events,
scaled in "psychological logarithm" units. As described in the previous
chapter, subjects were asked to mark each of six milestones on the line,
from the first passing thought of a possible offence, no matter how
brief, through stages of consideration and planning, to the point of
inevitability, when the offence was effectively in process and could not
easily have been averted. Several questions in the interview asked for
similar information, as a check on the quality of the data provided by
the timeline, and still other questions gathered further detail on
events in the offence process, such as reactions to thoughts about the
possibility of a new offence.

The results from the six points on the timeline, as summarized in
Table 3.9, provide some significant insight into the offence process.
The impulsive nature of many criminal offenses has long been
known, but these data provide some concrete representation of the
phenomenon.

Even the earliest landmark shows how little anticipation there was,
that is, the majority of subjects claimed that they had not experienced
even the first thought of an offence until they were virtually involved in
the crime – or at least within 15 minutes of its occurrence. Thus, for
over half, the entire process, from first passing thought or impulse to
commission of the crime, was collapsed into an hour or so; less than

Table 3.9. *Landmarks in offence planning*

	Point on timeline (percentage of subjects)					
	A	B	C	D	E	F
A month or more	12.2	6.9	4.0	2.3	1.3	0.3
A week or more	6.9	6.6	5.2	4.0	3.1	0.7
A day or more	11.9	11.9	10.6	9.3	8.6	3.7
Hours (1–24)	8.2	8.0	7.3	5.0	4.5	4.0
Minutes (< 1 hr)	7.0	8.3	7.9	7.3	6.6	3.3
At offence	53.8	58.4	65.0	72.1	75.8	88.1

Notes: A = first passing thought; B = first longer thought – at least 1 minute; C = first considered might actually do offence; D = first thought of planning, details or means; E = first definite planning; F = point of no return.

one in five subjects was aware of even the first thought of a possible offence as much as a week in advance.

As one moves along the continuum of points in the preoffence sequence, the numbers become even more concentrated at times nearer to the offence. For example, only about one in five said that they had planned any aspect of the offence or its commission more than an hour in advance.

The pattern of results provides some validation for our ordering of events in the sequence. More important, it emphasizes the lack of rational advance consideration. As we expected, the point of no return is very close to the time of the offence, because this point is more or less the actual beginning of the offence, for example, the time when a person walks into a store he intends to rob. However, it is somewhat surprising that other parts in the sequence are not further removed, or that so few subjects did any real planning, or that even noncommittal anticipatory thoughts are not reported as having occurred earlier.

These results are not dependent on the timeline technique of inquiry, but rather they are duplicated in the results of specific questions in the interview. For example, in response to a direct question 54.4% of subjects said that they had first thought of the offence at the time it occurred, a figure almost identical to that from the timeline data in Table 3.9.

Table 3.10. *Various offence measures*

Measure	Percentage
Never rehearsed offence	82.4
Never planned before offence	83.4
Never daydreamed about offence	88.7
Anything particular happen before first thought?	84.8
Difficulties in living related to offence?	82.1
Aware something happening at first chance?	56.3
How handled first impulse:	
Active: self-control, get help	2.6
Passive: don't resist, ignore, nothing	13.2
Act on it	71.8
Begin planning	5.2
Ever think of good consequences of offence?	54.8
Thought of material gain	41.1
Thought of peer esteem	1.9
Thought of power	2.7
Thought of self-esteem	0.3
Thought of other	8.6
Ever think of bad consequences of offence?	38.9
Ever think of victim?	22.5

Other questions in the interview provide confirmatory detail, as summarized in Table 3.10, and in some further results not in the table. In response to a question about the total time they had planned for the offence, 83.4% said that they had not done any planning at all before it occurred, and only 11.1% reported planning for more than an hour. Very few (11.3%) said that they had ever daydreamed or fantasized about the offence in advance, and only 4.8% said that they had done so often. However, this was not because of any attempts at inhibition or self-control, for very few said that they had failed to daydream about the offence because of its possible negative consequences; most answers to the question on this point were to the effect that "it just didn't happen that way."

Although planning and anticipation were generally sparse, subjects had still been to some extent aware of possible consequences of their actions, even though they were obviously not well deterred. A strong minority said that they had thought of the negative consequences before they acted. Many had even thought of the victim in advance, although we were admittedly remiss in failing to ask for more detail here. (Among other things, our question "Did you ever think of the victim?" is ambiguous. For example, it has a meaning that we did not intend for offenders who assaulted a particular person for revenge.)

Perhaps the thoughts of negative consequences had little effect because they were countered by stronger or more numerous thoughts of positive effects of the offence. Such benefits had occurred to the majority of subjects, more than had thought of possible negative effects, raising the possibility that they had deliberately used such thoughts to bolster their resolve. In most cases, the benefit specified was some sort of material gain, leading us to expect that this sort of anticipation occurred principally with property offences, a hypothesis that will be evaluated in a later chapter.

Whatever the anticipatory thoughts, in most cases the offence sequence occurred quickly, and there is evidence that it may prove very difficult to interrupt the process once the earliest components begin. For example, three-quarters of subjects had dealt with the very first impulse to commit an offence by acting immediately or by planning for action soon after. For those who had not yielded to the first temptation, by far the most common response was to go with the flow by doing nothing or attempting to ignore the impulse, strategies that had no foreseeable way of aborting the sequence. Thus, one might say that the offence was effectively launched once the first anticipatory thoughts had occurred.

Other information indicates that it would have been difficult to interrupt the sequence (from thoughts to action) once it had started. In discussing the offence during the interview, we asked subjects whether there was a point where they could have stopped. Two out of five answered that once things had started they were not in control, and half of the remainder said that they had been in control at the start of the sequence but had lost it somewhere along the way, usually near the beginning. Once a man enters the final part of the offence path, events seem to unfold autonomously, even automatically.

Still, if subjects had been out of control or unable to stop, they were still at some level aware of what was happening. As can be seen in Table

3.10, most said that the first thoughts of the offence came after recognizing some particular difficulty in their lives, and that they thought the occurrence of the offence was related to problems they were experiencing. Thus, whether or not they controlled events, they did have information that could have been – but had not been – used as warning signals.

Conclusion

The message that emerges is consistent across a variety of measures and areas of subjects' lives. Living outside of prison was difficult for most of them. Not only were they subject to the usual variety of hassles, impediments, and problems that life presents for most of us, but their recent release from prison presented special difficulties, including reacculturation in a fast-changing society, social reintegration, and the many steps in establishing a new, lawful, permanent identify, such as residence and bank accounts. In addition, for this sample especially, there were difficulties with finding employment in a time of serious economic recession.

On the other hand, many recidivists engendered at least some of their own difficulties, such as the frequent interpersonal conflicts, by their woefully inadequate coping abilities; even without serious problems they were able to create their own. One may see their problems as imposed by society, or else as hardships they had themselves created by their personal inadequacies and by their chronic maladaptive behaviors, including criminal acts. Whatever one's attribution of responsibility, it is likely that the longer a man's prior record the more difficult the tasks of reintegration and establishing a new life would be.

As a result of their problems, the predominant moods were dysphoric, with depression, anxiety, frustration, and anger very common. The analogy to the breakdown process that has been demonstrated for alcoholic relapse seems to be supported by the evidence.

One of the most interesting aspects of our data is the evidence for dynamic changes during the preoffence period. For many subjects, there appears to have been a downward trend in moods and the tenor of their thoughts about their lives. There is also evidence for emotional changes, with a shift toward anger for some. The changes are particularly visible for those who had been released less than a month before their new offence, because our measurements captured the entire period of their release. However, we believe that similar patterns occurred for other subjects as well, and that the deteriorative changes were largely responsible for the relapse into recidivism.

After the euphoria and unrealistic expectations attendant on their initial release, the reality of their situations soon led to dysphoria. The trigger for relapse may have come when they arrived at an attribution about the source of their unhappiness, or a "solution" to their difficulties, or when they broke down otherwise under the stress. Regardless of exactly how the process ends, the existence of certain antecedents appears to be observable, and the data support the assertion that there are recognizable precursors to reoffending.

On the other hand, our data about the offence process itself indicate that, once initiated, the time course for offences is on the average even more foreshortened than has been previously demonstrated. The (re)initiation of offending may not be spontaneous, but once begun the process is often so quick that it is effectively autonomous. Often, once the offender has thought of an offence as an available option in his situation, its commission is perhaps already inevitable, and successful intervention is already precluded.

We cannot say for certain whether this process actually occurs as described. Given the possibilities of retrospective distortion and limits even to undistorted recall, our data have imperfect reliable detail, and they must be interpreted cautiously. Only a longitudinal study that follows dynamic factors prospectively from the time of release can provide a truly definitive picture of the sequence of events in the recidivism process. However, the information educed here on both the precursors of recidivism and the offence process itself constitutes an advance on previous knowledge, and in themselves the results are good evidence for a breakdown model, even though we have only limited direct information on the sequencing of elements.

However, this conclusion is still premature. Although there is face validity to the claim that some special features of subjects' lives on the outside lead to reoffending, we have not yet established that they really differ from any other population. The comparisons with our control group in the next chapter will address this question.

In addition, it should be noted that there was much variability in many of our measures. This may indicate that there were several determinative paths operative at the same time, and that the general picture of the path to recidivism given here is a composite of several subpopulations that blurs many of the details. We shall attempt to shed some light on this question as well when we look later at comparisons across offence groups.

CHAPTER FOUR

Comparisons with Nonrecidivists

ALTHOUGH THE INFORMATION on behavior of reoffenders in the community allows us to construct a picture of recidivists' lifestyles, moods, and outlooks that has some use in understanding criminal behavior generally, the data presented so far do not allow us to address questions of proximal causation very effectively. On the basis of the data, we cannot say which events actually influence the commission of new offences, and which are epiphenomenal. For example, high rates of unemployment or of depression may be determinative of recidivism, or they may be characteristic of marginal populations, or of people who have recently undergone major transitions in their lives. Moreover, some of the specifics of the results may have been produced by features of the method of inquiry. In short, conclusions are impossible without information on comparative or marginal rates.

Our group of men who had been released and who had not reoffended provides comparative data. Any area in which this group does not differ from the set of recidivists is unlikely to be a precursor of renewed offending. The use of this comparison group does not control for all possible confounding variables, but it does match recent past experience of imprisonment and release, and it will allow us to narrow the broad picture shown in the preceding chapter. Although the comparison group is relatively small in comparison to the recidivist group, it is large enough to allow statistical comparisons, certainly where differences are sizeable or consistent. As will be seen, there are substantial group differences on a great many types of measures.

69

Unless otherwise indicated, the statistical comparisons used either *F* or *t*-tests, for continuous variables, or chi-square, for categorical data. Occasionally, categories of a nominal variable are combined or collapsed in the results included here; this was normally done only after initial comparisons showed significant differences using exhaustive categorizations. If distributions on a given variable were badly skewed they were transformed before statistical comparisons, but untransformed means are shown in the text or tables. Tests of significance are included in the text only for measures not included in tables; for information in the tables, only the level of significance is indicated.

Personal and Criminal History

We looked first at a variety of historical measures that have previously been shown to be associated with recidivism or with extensive criminal histories. As can be seen in Table 4.1, there were extensive differences between the two groups. Recidivists had led more unstable lives than nonrecidivists, although they did not appear to have been more troubled generally. Recidivists had experienced more problems at school and dropped out earlier. They had moved around more frequently, held jobs for shorter times, and did not maintain relationships as long. Some of this might have been because recidivists were younger, but differences were also apparent even when only the older recidivists were included.

At the same time, indices of maladjustment did not significantly differentiate the groups. If anything, nonrecidivists tended to report more previous psychological problems (even more suicidal thoughts), and a greater proportion had received professional treatment. However, the only differences that are statistically reliable are on measures of a history of substance abuse, where the recidivists clearly had more difficulties. For example, on a list of alcohol-derived problems in seven areas included in the LSI, recidivists reported a mean of 3.2 while the others had only 1.4 ($F(1,335) = 24.69$, $p < .001$).

There were also differences in criminal history, as shown in the bottom part of Table 4.1. The recidivists had been in trouble with the law at a younger age and had longer and more violent criminal histories. The total LSI score shows that the recidivists were at greater

Table 4.1. *Personal and criminal history measures*

Measure	Recidivists	Nonrecidivists
Personal		
Age	29.5	42.3[a]
Highest school grade	9.5	10.3[b]
Had problems at school	44.7%	28.6%
Other family criminal	51.0%	34.3%
Longest time lived in same place (mos)	27.2	62.6[a]
No more than 6 months	25.8%	8.6%
Longest time held same job (mos)	26.4	63.6[a]
No more than 6 months	31.3%	8.3%
Longest heterosexual relationship (mos)	37.2	87.8[a]
No more than 6 months	25.2%	25.0%
Ever had any psychological problems	61.2%	72.2%
Ever treated on outside	38.6%	54.0%
Saw psychologist in prison	39.0%	51.4%
Ever had substance abuse problem	80.0%	41.7%[a]
Ever treated	52.6%	40.5%
Had considered suicide	25.5%	40.3%[b]
Criminal		
Total prior convictions	25.0	14.8[b]
Violent prior offences	3.5	1.4[b]
No violent offences	32.2%	58.3%
Age at first trouble with the law	14.6	20.8[a]
Younger than 18 at first trouble	82.9%	50.0%
LSI (max 50)	28.2	19.2[a]
Time out before reimprisonment[c] (mos)	7.5	29.1[a]

[a] $p < .001$
[b] $p < .05$
[c] For nonrecidivists, time out before interview.

risk of reoffending than the comparison group. This appears to have been recognized within the correctional system, because almost 80% of the nonrecidivists had been released from minimum-security institutions, as compared to less than one-third of recidivists ($X^2(1) = 31.2$, $p < .001$). The LSI Criminal Subscale, which provides a summary of criminal history, showed differences between the groups

(M = 4.2 for nonrecidivists vs. 7.1 for recidivists; $F(1,345)$ = 155.49, $p < .001$).

On first thought, these differences might be seen as disappointing, because they show that the groups are not well matched on personal history. On second consideration, we must remember that a great deal of previous research has shown that recidivism can be predicted from factors such as previous criminal history. It is therefore not surprising that the same factors retrospectively differentiate samples of recidivists and nonrecidivists. To obtain a closer match on historical factors, one would need to find habitual offenders who were making a break with their past and who would not reoffend, but criminal career data show how infrequently this occurs. In any case, it should be noted that the nonrecidivist group did have serious and lengthy criminal histories, even if they were on the average shorter than those for recidivists. (We will address the matter of these historical differences again later in this chapter, when we use analyses of covariance to remove the effects of criminal history from other measures.)

An even stronger argument may be advanced regarding any supposed importance of differences in criminal history. One of the primary hypotheses of this research is that the resumption of criminal behavior is largely precipitated by contemporary events in offenders' lives. If this is so, that is, if the determinants of new offences are in the immediate behavior patterns, then chronic behavior patterns would over time lead to different histories. In particular, such things as criminal history would reflect the accumulated long-term influence of chronic maladaptive behaviors. In effect, then, we can argue that differences in criminal history between our groups do not *explain* the fact of recidivism or nonrecidivism, but rather that the lengthier criminal history in our recidivist group is the eventual *result* of differences in the ways that recidivists habitually behave and respond to situations.

Lifestyle in the Community

We are led to consider next the differences between the groups on measures of general behavior and lifestyle outside of prison. Table 4.2 summarizes a number of differences. Measures for recidivists are for the preoffence period, while for nonrecidivists they cover a period of comparable length preceding the interview. On the average, the lives

Table 4.2. *Outside lifestyle measures*

Measure	Recidivists	Non-recidivists
Living in nuclear family?	28.4%	47.2[a]
Marital status:		
Currently married (including common-law)	35.1%	44.5%
Single	46.3%	41.6%
Other (separated, homosexual, unknown)	18.7%	13.9%
Currently working (including part time)	42.1%	61.1%[a]
Principal source of income:[b]		
Employment	34.2%	41.7%
Government benefits	32.6%	55.5%
Illegal activity	22.3%	0.0%
Other (family, friends, etc.)	11.0%	2.8%
Time use – mean proportion of time specified in:		
Family activities	12.4	19.8[a]
Hobbies	5.2	11.7[b]
Listening to music	25.3	16.1[a]
Watching TV	16.1	26.3[b]
Physical activity	9.2	9.0
Hanging around	19.5	7.0[b]
Criminal Socialization Scale (max = 7)	1.9	2.8[b]
Social Isolation Subscale (max = 9)	2.4	1.5[c]
Time Use/Time Framing Scale	14.6	17.5[b]
Worried life not going the way he wanted?	79.0%	52.8[c]
Rate life (1–100)	44.6	67.5[c]
Mean confidence about success on outside	2.3	1.4[c]

[a] $p < .05$
[b] $p < .01$
[c] $p < .001$

of the nonrecidivists seem to have been much more conventional and mundane than those of the recidivists. They were significantly more likely to be employed, and they were also more likely to be living as a parent in a nuclear family. Those who were not working full time almost all had a regular source of income from either unemployment insurance (22%) or welfare (33%), rather than living off the proceeds of illegal behavior.

Similar differences are also visible in our survey of how subjects used their time. For the nonrecidivists, the heaviest investment of time was in watching TV and family activities, while for the recidivists more time was spent in listening to music or just "hanging out" with friends. The proportions of time specified differed significantly in every category except physical activities.

Thus, reoffenders showed much time in the casual unstructured socialization with acquaintances that is characteristic of male adolescent peer groups and that has been described previously as characteristic of offenders. These differences are seen in the significant differences on our Criminal Socialization Scale. On the other hand, reoffenders were also more likely to be isolated, as shown by our Social Isolation Scale.

In summary, it would appear that the nonrecidivists led lives that were more conventional and also more organized. They showed more concern with their use of time, as demonstrated by differences on the Time Use and Time Framing Scale. Not surprisingly, they were less frequently bored ($M = 2.0$ vs. 2.8 on a five-point scale; $F(1,345) = 7.81, p < .01$).

Differences in generalized cognitions about their lives accompany these lifestyle differences between groups. Specifically, on a variety of measures recidivists appear to have been less happy with their lives. Among other things, they were more likely to feel that their lives had not been going the way they wanted, and they also rated the quality of their lives much lower than did the nonrecidivists. Although these reports may have been colored or exaggerated in light of later events, they are strongly consistent with other information. One would expect that a man's global appraisals are a summary of his outlook on life, so these findings show important differences between the groups in their outlook on life.

Problems and Coping

In addition to differences in the general pattern of behavior, recidivists appraised and dealt with the problems they faced on the outside quite differently than did nonrecidivists. Results from selected measures are shown in Table 4.3. Even on the first inquiry about problems, recidivists seemed to have more problems in living outside of prison than did nonrecidivists. Although the comparison periods certainly differ, recency probably favored recall of relatively unimportant problems for the nonrecidivists. Nevertheless, the majority were unable to mention any significant problems in response to the first general inquiry, whereas almost all of the reoffenders listed at least one problem without prompting. This difference was not owing to availability of problem areas in memory: Even in response to our specific prompting about possible problem areas, the recidivists appear to have perceived more problems, about twice as many as the comparison group.

Perhaps more important than the number of problems are the frequencies of certain types of problems. There were significant differences between groups in the frequency of interpersonal conflicts, complications from substance abuse, and financial difficulties. Recidivists did not mention unemployment more frequently as a problem, despite their higher rate of unemployment.

Other measures of perceived problems yielded similar and confirmatory information. The three types of problems that differed on the problem survey were also each significantly different in the timeline data. However, the timeline data also differed in the category of (un)employment problems. The latter is likely the result of the method used in reading the timelines: If a subject mentioned unemployment on the "events" line, it was always counted as a problem. In contrast, in the problem survey, unemployment was counted only if the subject himself explicitly identified it as a problem. This method difference again indicates that many recidivists did not see their lack of employment as a problem. In addition to the frequency data, assessments of problem seriousness in each of nine areas showed significantly higher ratings by recidivists in every category except for problems from work or lack of it, with the largest differences in categories covering interpersonal conflicts and substance abuse.

Thus, the recidivists appeared to have seen more problems in their lives, and they appraised the problems they did have as more serious than did the nonrecidivists. Several different types of measures independently and congruently indicate that the problem areas that differentiated the groups best were interpersonal conflict and substance abuse.

Table 4.3. *Problems experienced after release*

Measure	Recidivists	Nonrecidivists
Problems mentioned at first inquiry:		
Interpersonal conflict	25.2%	5.6%[a]
Substance abuse	21.3%	2.8%[a]
Money/financial	18.1%	2.8%[b]
Work/school/unemployment	11.9%	16.7%
None at all	12.3%	61.1%[c]
Mean total number mentioned after listing		
and search (possible 17)	3.6	2.0[c]
Problematic events mentioned on timeline:		
Interpersonal	38.4%	6.1%[c]
Substance (ab)use	33.4%	0.0%[c]
Money	23.7%	6.1%[b]
(Un)employment	20.5%	6.1%[b]
Parole or supervision	7.1%	0.0
Feelings/moods	8.1%	2.8%
Mean problem seriousness ratings (0–10):		
Substance abuse	5.4	0.3[c]
Money/financial	4.9	3.3[b]
Work/school	4.3	3.0
Physical or emotional health	3.9	1.6[c]
Wife or family	3.5	0.9[c]
Release supervision	3.5	1.7[a]
Housing or living situation	2.7	1.4[b]
Friends	2.6	0.7[c]
Time (boredom, activities available, etc.)	2.6	1.0[a]

[a] $p < .05$
[b] $p < .01$
[c] $p < .001$

Not only did they have more problems, but the recidivist group also had coping skills that were less effective than those of the nonrecidivist survivors. This can be seen in our overall measure of coping efficacy ($M = 10.4$ vs. 11.6; $F(1,273) = 8.89$, $p < .01$), and also in significant differences in scores for three of the individual situations comprising the total. The largest difference was on the situation describing a conflict with a spouse (M = 10.7 vs. 11.9; $F(1,265)$ = 6.66, $p < .05$). Scores also significantly differentiated the nonrecidivists on scenarios describing an opportunity to go to a party on a work night, and dealing with loneliness after release from prison.

Still, from their responses neither group seemed particularly effective in remediating problematic situations, and even the scores for the nonrecidivist sample did not approach those of a noncriminal group (e.g., Hughes and Zamble, 1993). What may be more diagnostic of probable trouble are scores on our risk scale, indexing possible exacerbation or risk of new problems arising from the coping responses used. On this measure, two-thirds of the recidivists were assigned a risk score on at least one situation, twice the proportion for the nonrecidivists ($F(1,273)$ = 4.51, $p < .05$). If neither group was able to solve their problems well, the recidivists were still far more likely to make small problems more serious, or to create new problems for themselves. The differences in level of coping skills between the groups are important to the arguments advanced in this book because they are theoretically linked to the existence and magnitude of problems hypothesized to be central to the process of recidivism. Methodologically, the assessments of coping are minimally subject to retrospective bias, if at all.

The differences in both coping efficacy and perceived problems are combined in our measure of coping adequacy, calculated as the ratio of coping efficacy to the number of problems. As expected, the differences on this measure are particularly strong ($F(1,269)$ = 14.74, $p < .001$).

In summary, we can say that recidivists perceived more problems and were also less able to cope successfully. There likely was some causal relationship between problems and coping skills, because respondents had the capacity to create problems by their reactions to ordinary situations. In support of this claim, we note that the problems that occurred most frequently, and that distinguished recidivists from control subjects most strongly, were the types most likely to be self-created, like interpersonal conflict or substance abuse. The lives of many reoffenders were thus distinctive in the period leading up to the resumption of criminal behavior.

Given the expected differences in substance abuse, specific and quantitative measures of alcohol and drug consumption in the

preoffence period elaborated on information from the problem surveys, with results as summarized in Table 4.4. The nonreoffenders
were not as a rule abstainers, with about half reporting some amount
of alcohol use in the period of interest, and a minority even admit-
ting to illegal drug use. However, the reported amounts and frequencies of nonrecidivists' use show almost universal moderation.

More recidivists used alcohol regularly, and when they did they
drank much more. More recidivists took prohibited drugs, and when
they did they ingested much more frequently. The differences appear
in each period surveyed. The level of substance abuse is unquestion-
ably a major factor that differentiates our subject groups. (It is possible
that some nonrecidivist subjects may not have been honest in answering questions about substance abuse, because the terms of their conditional release included total abstinence. In general, we believe that
our pledge of confidentiality was understood and returned with can-
dor, but we cannot assess the extent to which subjects gave incorrect
information. If they did so anywhere, it would most likely be in the area
of substance abuse. However, given the consistency of answers, and the
entire pattern of the data, we believe that there is no reason to
seriously doubt the results on this issue.)

Emotions

Given our expectations about the relationship between inadequate
coping and dysphoric emotional reactions, and about the role of those
responses in relapse into maladaptive behavioral patterns, the comparisons between groups on reports of moods and emotions are particularly important. In this case, reports by recidivists of emotions in the
preoffence period were compared to reports by nonrecidivists for the
period before the interview.

Comparisons for selected measures are shown in Table 4.5. There
are considerable differences even on the most general measure,
namely, all strong emotional states reported for the 30-day period
preceding either the offence or the interview, with differences on
every dysphoric feeling except for "stressed." The combined summary measure of all dysphoric states showed high percentages in each
group, as expected given the range of emotions and the length of the
period, but even so there was a sizeable difference between the groups.

Table 4.4. *Alcohol and drug use*

Measure	Recidivists	Nonrecidivists
Substance abuse visible on timeline	37.3%	3.0%[a]
Alcohol Dependency Scale	8.3	2.9[b]
Drug Abuse Screening Test	6.6	1.8[c]
General preoffence period:[d]		
Using alcohol	80.3%	47.1%[b]
Averaging at least 6 drinks daily	26.5%	0.0[b]
Daily intake (standard units) for drinkers	7.5	0.9[a]
Alcohol increases violence	21.0%	5.9%[c]
Using any other drugs illegally	63.2%	14.7%[a]
Using daily	29.6%	0.0
Number of different drugs for users	1.6	1.4
Days/month users take any drugs	19.1	5.4[c]
Last day (24 hrs) before offence:[d]		
Using any alcohol	56.0%	16.7%[a]
At least 6 drinks	42.4%	2.8%[a]

[a] $p < .05$
[b] $p < .01$
[c] $p < .001$
[d] For nonrecidivists, period is before interview.

Similarly, the frequency of occurrence of at least one of the three most common clinical dysphoric states was more than twice as high for recidivists.

The pattern of results for the strongest single emotion in the 30-day period (not shown in the table) is very similar. For example, frequencies on the general dysphoric summary measure were 77.2% for recidivists and 41.7% for nonrecidivists ($X^2(1) = p < .001$), while in contrast 58.3% of the nonrecidivists and only 17.9% of recidivists said that their predominant state was positive ($X^2(1) = 31.17, p < .001$).

In the shorter measurement period of 48 hours before the respective reference points, some differences between groups appear even greater, as values for the nonrecidivist group fall to zero. As may be seen in Table 4.5, of the 10 dysphoric states, only guilt and boredom fail to differentiate the groups statistically, and even here the lack of

Table 4.5. *Strong emotions in preoffence period (percentages)*

	In 30 days		In 48 hours	
Emotional State	Recidivists	Nonrecidivists	Recidivists	Nonrecidivists
Hopelessness	17.5	0.0[a]	12.3	0.0[b]
Depression	38.2	11.8[a]	24.3	0.0[a]
Moody/brooding	18.1	0.0[a]	12.3	0.0[b]
Anger	31.1	11.8[b]	27.5	0.0[c]
Frustration	39.8	11.8[a]	30.7	5.9[a]
Stressed	27.5	20.6	19.7	2.9[b]
Anxiety	35.6	11.8[a]	23.9	5.9[b]
Guilt	15.9	0.0[b]	7.4	0.0
Loneliness	22.7	2.9[a]	14.6	0.0[b]
Boredom	23.6	2.9[a]	11.4	5.9
Sexual frustration	5.2	0.0	3.9	0.0
Nothing/numb	11.7	0.0[b]	10.7	0.0[b]
Positive (all)	35.6	70.6[c]	29.8	88.2[c]
Any dysphoric[d]	79.7	47.2[c]	67.8	11.1[c]
Major dysphoric[e]	62.7	27.8[c]	52.7	5.6[c]

Questionnaire measures	Recidivists	Nonrecidivists
Beck Depression Inventory	17.0	4.5[c]
Percent moderate or severe (19 or higher)	40.4	3.0
Spielberger State Anxiety	48.6	31.8[c]
Score 46 or higher	56.1%	9.1%
Multimodal Anger Inventory Subscales		
Anger Arousal	17.5	11.8[c]
Anger Expression	22.5	19.5[b]
Hostility	11.6	9.0[c]
Anger In	13.2	10.1[c]
Anger Out	6.1	5.8

[a] $p < .05$
[b] $p < .01$
[c] $p < .001$
[d] One or more of the first 10 listed states, from hopelessness to boredom.
[e] One or more of depression, anger, or anxiety.

significance is largely because of low rates. The summary measure for all dysphoric states combined shows rates about six times as high among recidivists. If we count only the major clinical dysphoric states, the ratio is almost 10 to 1.

Differences for the strongest single emotion in the shorter period (omitted from the table) are very similar. Only 11.1% of nonrecidivists selected any negative states (in every case either frustration or boredom), as compared to 65.0% of the recidivists ($X^2(1) = 38.77$, $p < .001$). None of the nonrecidivists chose any of the major clinical states, but 37.6% of reoffenders did so ($X^2(1) = 20.43$, $p < .001$). The figures for positive states were complementary: 83.3% of nonrecidivists said that their predominant mood was positive, in contrast to only 21.1% of recidivists ($X^2(1) = 63.25$, $p < .001$).

Alternative measures of emotional states show much the same thing. Frequencies for individual states listed on the timeline do not discriminate as well as the interview results, because of generally reduced rates. Still, depression, anger, and frustration are each significantly more frequent for recidivists. Specification of some dysphoric state was more than twice as likely for recidivists ($X^2(1) = 26.33$, $p < .001$), and a listing of one of the major dysphoric triad was three times as likely ($X^2(1) = 20.26$, $p < .001$).

Questionnaire measures also showed more long-standing anger, anxiety, and depression among recidivists. Even the questions about emotional responses to the situations depicted in the coping scenarios showed more frequent anger ($F(1,293) = 5.36$, $p < .05$) and depression ($F(1,293) = 6.89$, $p < .01$). Thus, the tendencies to react emotionally in certain ways are probably generalized across at least certain types of problem situations, rather than being specific to the circumstances of individual subjects in the preoffence period.

In summary, each measure of emotional responses states indicates that the substantial incidence of emotional problems reported by recidivists in the preoffence period is not characteristic of exoffenders and is almost certainly not the result of biases in the interview or testing procedures. It is likely that the differences show some general tendencies to react to stressful situations with negative moods. We find it difficult to avoid the conclusion that strong dysphoria is linked to the commission of new offences.

Moreover, negative emotional states seem linked to problems that subjects were experiencing – or at least they thought this was so. When we asked them what had set off their (mostly negative) feelings in the preoffence (preinterview) period, groups differed significantly in the choices of three specific categories, interpersonal problems, lack of money, and substance abuse. The largest difference was in the interpersonal category, which was cited by 37.4% of recidivists and only 5.6% of nonrecidivists ($X^2(1) = 14.49$, $p < .001$).

Thoughts

Given the picture of behavior above, it is not surprising that there are also differences in the things that subjects recalled as having occupied their thoughts. As summarized in Table 4.6, nonrecidivists' thoughts about specific matters most frequently concerned their work – or lack of work for those unemployed. In contrast, reoffenders were more likely to be concerned with money and drug or alcohol use. High proportions of men in each group were also concerned with interpersonal relationships, but the difference was not statistically significant. Finally, thoughts of a subsequent criminal offence were cited by some recidivists but none of the nonrecidivists, quite expectably.

Global thoughts also differed. Far more nonrecidivists reported at least some generally positive or optimistic ideation. Similarly, none of the nonrecidivists reported negative global thoughts, but about one in nine recidivists did so.

There were also some interesting differences in changes across the period, as indexed by our assessment of overall trends on the timeline. About four in five of the nonrecidivists had patterns that were assessed as even and level, as compared to only 30% of the recidivists. Most of the rest of the nonrecidivists (18%) were classified as showing a positive trend, but less than 2% of recidivists. In contrast, 68% of the recidivists were classified as showing patterns that were either uniformly negative or changing for the worse, as compared to only one individual (3%) in the nonrecidivist group. Overall, the pattern differences are statistically quite reliable ($X^2(3) = 60.93$, $p < .001$). Thus, there is no evidence of generally negative or deteriorating moods among the nonrecidivists to match what we see for recidivists.

Although the reliability of these classifications has not been assessed, they were done blind, that is, without knowledge of group

Table 4.6. *Thoughts in preoffence period (from timeline)*

Category	Mentioned anywhere in the period (percentage)	
	Recidivists	Nonrecidivists
Interpersonal	48.0	38.2
Money	23.7	5.9[a]
Substance (ab)use	31.5	2.9[b]
Employment	35.4	73.5[b]
Parole/authorities	18.3	12.5
Criminal – instrumental	11.7	0.0[a]
Criminal – emotive	5.5	2.9
Return to prison	10.1	0.0
Reform/self-improvement	11.0	20.6
Positive/optimistic	16.6	58.9[b]
General negative cognitions	11.4	0.0[a]

[a] $p < .05$
[b] $p < .001$

membership. The differences are so considerable that they almost certainly transcend any unreliability of classification or imprecision in the category definitions. Before their offences, recidivists had found problems they could not deal with effectively, and their moods and thoughts were becoming increasingly negative. But there were no similar changes or effects among exoffenders who were surviving without committing new offences. It is reasonable to conclude that the lives of reoffenders – or at least their perceptions of their own lives – were generally distinctive in the period leading up to the resumption of criminal behavior.

Analyses of Covariance

The discussion in the preceding sections has concentrated on differences in antecedents to recidivism, mostly ignoring the differences that were also found in historical measures. However, given that both types of differences exist, one could argue that the personal and historical factors are primary, and that the apparent effects in the current dynamic measures can be attributed to those prior differences. A great deal of our argument would then be built of phantom bricks.

To evaluate this type of reasoning, we repeated most of our prior analyses using analyses of covariance. In the first analyses of this kind, the effects of the total number of criminal convictions and age were covaried out (that is, removed statistically) before the significance of differences in any dependent measure was calculated. Thus, these analyses determine whether differences remain between recidivists and nonrecidivists after correcting for the prior effects of age and criminal history.

The results are unequivocal: The essential differences remain. In some ways, the picture of differences in the antecedents of offending is even sharpened. Table 4.7 summarizes tests of significance for representative variables from each of the preceding sections, with redundant or overlapping measures omitted.

When we control for age and criminal history, the majority of other differences in background and history are no longer significant, indicating that any differences that were apparent in the uncorrected analyses are the result of age and/or previous record. The lack of any remaining significant differences also indicates that the covariates chosen are generally sufficient to subsume the variance attributable to historical variables. (The number of pervious violent offences is a notable exception that we shall deal with shortly.) Some of the apparent differences in lifestyle also disappear; for example, only one category of time use is still significantly different across groups. Thus, although background and lifestyle factors may be instrumental in the origin of offending, they do not in themselves allow us to reliably distinguish who will become recidivists.

In contrast, specific aspects of behavior, such as patterns of socialization or drug and alcohol use, still consistently differ reliably between the groups. Most of the significant differences in these types of measures that we have reviewed in Tables 4.2 to 4.6 are still significant. For example, reoffenders still perceive more (and more serious) problems in several categories, especially interpersonal difficulties and substance abuse. The one change when we control for age and criminal history is that there is no longer a difference in money problems, no matter how we measure it. In addition, there are still differences in a variety of emotional responses, as well as in

Table 4.7. *Selected significant differences after controlling for age and criminal history*

Variable	F
Highest school grade	1.68
Longest lived in same place	1.15
Age at first trouble with the law	1.76
Violent prior offences	11.26[a]
Previous psychological problems	0.38
Currently working	1.77
Time use – mean proportion of time specified in:	
Family activities	1.78
Hobbies	9.71[b]
Hanging out	2.30
Criminal Socialization Scale	7.81[b]
Criminal Isolation Scale	14.28[a]
Time Use and Time Framing Scale	3.08
Worried life not going the way he wanted?	11.08[a]
Rate life (1–100)	15.26[a]
Mean problem seriousness ratings (0–10)	
Substance abuse	45.34[a]
Money/financial	2.42
Work/school	0.12
Physical or emotional health	17.39[a]
Wife or family	9.17[b]
Release supervision	9.68[b]
Friends	8.90[b]
Time (boredom, activities available, etc.)	9.88[b]
Using alcohol in preoffence period[d]	15.24[a]
Daily alcohol intake	6.15[c]
Using any other drugs illegally	23.85[a]
Emotional state in 48 hours preoffence[d]	
Depressed	7.42[c]
Anger	6.85[b]
Frustration	3.47
Anxiety	2.64
Loneliness	8.67[b]
Bored	0.80
Positive	36.54[a]
Any dysphoric	32.94[a]

[a] $p < .001$
[b] $p < .01$
[c] $p < .05$
[d] For nonrecidivists, period is before interview.

such measures as coping adequacy ($F(1,245) = 14.74$, $p < .01$), or the changes over time in mood and cognitions ($F(1,306) = 37.20$, $p < .001$).

From the first set of covariate analyses, one can see that a difference in the number of previous violent convictions persists, and it could affect results with other measures. Therefore, we performed another set of analyses with previous violent convictions added as a third covariate. Although a few marginal differences slipped to nonsignificant levels (and a few went the other way) the pattern of significant effects remains as we have described.

Finally, we looked at the influence of social desirability, by adding our questionnaire measure of socially desirable responding as a third covariate in addition to age and criminal convictions. Social desirability was a significant covariate for many measures, probably more than the other variables controlled for, but its effect on the overall pattern of significant effects was generally insubstantial. For example, the only measure from Table 4.7 that changes from clearly significant to clearly nonsignificant is the proportion of time spent in hobbies or other structured leisure time. Also, the measure of problems with friends now falls just short of significance, but other measures of interpersonal problems still show clear differences.

In summary, very few of the group differences apparent at first inspection appear to be confounds from covarying factors. When these effects are accounted for, the group differences central to our argument remain. At least some of the answers given by at least some subjects were influenced by a desire to give socially desirable responses, but even after this bias is removed there are still reliable differences between recidivists and nonrecidivists. Other apparent differences, such as the number of previous psychological problems, appear to be the result of age or criminal history, but when these effects are removed the central pattern of differences in current psychological state seems even more clear than before. We feel impelled to conclude that there is a coherent set of factors in the ongoing psychological processes of recidivists that sets them apart from other exoffenders.

Discriminant Analysis

From a statistical perspective, the plethora of differences between recidivists and nonrecidivists is almost an embarrassment. With so many redundant measures, it is difficult to assess how well they work together to distinguish – and, in other samples, to predict – who will commit new offences. In this respect, other types of multivariate analysis can be helpful.

A discriminant analysis was performed using the same set of 30 variables as described in Chapter 3. We should reiterate that each of these measures individually differed significantly between reoffenders and nonreoffenders, and that they were all observable antecedents to the new offences. In principle, an independent observer could monitor all of the specified behaviors on an ongoing basis, so the results have potential practical application.

The present analysis looked at a single aggregate predictor to see how each variable was weighted relative to the others. This can be quite informative for a theoretical model. Given that the resultant function could be used dynamically to predict reoffending for other releasees, the important practical question was how accurately it could classify recidivists and nonrecidivists from the present study. Accurate prediction in this case indicates at least the possibility of being able to correctly identify actual or potential recidivists in a new sample.

Table 4.8 shows the coefficients for each of the 30 variables in the discriminant function. The heaviest weightings seem to be spread across the several types of measures, with each type participating and none predominating. Thus, as we have been claiming, several different ongoing psychological processes work in combination to lead a person along the path to recidivism.

The classification results indicate that the function is a very accurate discriminator. Of the 311 recidivists, 309 were correctly classified; 28 of the 36 nonrecidivists were also correctly identified. The overall accuracy was thus in excess of 97%.

One cannot say to what extent the obtained function capitalizes on variance unique to the present sample. However, it is worth mentioning that approximately 40% of the sample had at least one missing data point among the 30 variables, which excluded them from the

Table 4.8. *Standardized canonical discriminant function coefficients*

Variable	Coefficient
Substance abuse problem	.2563
Emotional problem	−.0319
Interpersonal (family) problem	.0052
Money problem	−.0875
Supervisor problem	.1908
Previous psychological problems	−.3587
Anger in 24 hours preoffence	.0702
Anxiety in 24 hours preoffence	.0743
Depression in 24 hours preoffence	−.0843
Frustrated in 24 hours preoffence	.1561
Positive mood in 24 hours preoffence	−.2557
Beck Depression Inventory	.3188
Anger Arousal Subscale	.2202
Deteriorating outlook	.4630
Drinks in 24 hours preoffence	.2177
Days continuous drug use preoffence	.0595
Average daily drinks (FQI)	−.0251
Number of drug types used	.0799
Time Use Scale	.0807
Criminal Socialization Scale	−.0617
Social Isolation Scale	.5503
Social Desirability Scale	.0120
Frequency bored	−.1971
Thought of negative consequences	−.4167
Percent of time "hanging out"	.2793
Under supervision	−.2810
Employed	−.0844
Rating of quality of life	−.0659
Coping adequacy	−.1456

derivation of the discriminant function but not from the final classification. This can be viewed as a very informal sort of cross-validation; that is, the fact that most of the subjects with missing data are still correctly identified by the derived function indicates that the function could be used successfully to identify recidivists in a new population.

These data are promising but hardly conclusive. The results are likely affected by the disproportionate numbers in the two groups, and the accuracy of classification will likely be degraded in any replication, especially one done predictively. However, the classification data are at least strong intimations of practical utility for our model in the future.

Finally, it should be reiterated that the set of variables used in this analysis excludes measures of social and criminal history. We did try additional analyses with historical factors added to the variable set, and the accuracy of prediction was somewhat degraded. This may be relevant to some of the arguments in subsequent chapters.

Offences That Did Not Occur

Although there were major differences between groups in factors that our theoretical perspective says are linked to reoffending, it should be remembered that most of the nonrecidivists had extensive previous criminal histories. If one thinks of persistent offending as habitual, then new offences might be expected almost as a matter of course, regardless of conditions. Also, many had returned to old environments that might have contributed to their prior offences and where there were both expectations about their behavior and social support or encouragement for criminal activities. All of these might be expected to lead to new criminal offences. Combined with the frustrations and temptations of ordinary life, these predisposing conditions might be thought to induce some probability of reoffending, even if it had not eventuated by the time of our investigation.

Thus, we are led to consider what stopped these men from committing new offences. To pursue this line of inquiry, we had included several questions in the interview that asked nonrecidivists about their thoughts of possible new offences. These questions took the place of inquiries about steps in the offence process for recidivists.

Even the nonrecidivists reported occasions when there were possibilities that they might have reoffended. For example, about 35% said that there had been times within the preceding few months when they had been aware of at least some passing thoughts of a new offence.

While this indicates something far from universal vulnerability, one should remember that only about the same proportion of the recidivist group reported having been aware of any casual thoughts of their offence prior to its occurrence: If one counts events up to one day before their offence for recidivists, then the total is about 31%; if one includes all times up to an hour preoffence, then the sum still reaches only 39%.

However, after initial thoughts the process seemed to accelerate for recidivists, whereas the figures for further steps in the offence process fall off sharply for the control group. Only 17% said that they had ever daydreamed or fantasized about an offence. Despite the number who had entertained casual thoughts of criminal acts, only 6% said that there had ever been any serious possibility that they might actually commit an offence (less than one-third the proportion of reoffenders who remembered any similar awareness a day before offending).

One might then wonder why men in the comparison group did not proceed through the steps toward a new criminal offence, even though they were as likely to experience the first step as recidivists. Part of the answer seems to lie in how they reacted to thoughts of offending. In response to our question about what they did after their first thoughts, the largest proportions of nonrecidivists said that they had either ignored the thoughts or just done nothing (29% each), unlike the recidivists, most of whom began to act. This might be interpreted as passive resistance, or it might be that the impulses toward action were simply weaker for the nonrecidivists. While we have no direct evidence on the strength of impulses, we do have some indications that subjects in the comparison group were not passive in dealing with the temptations to which they were exposed. Rather, several pieces of information indicate an important role for thoughts invoking the possible negative consequences of criminal behavior.

We can see this first in answers to questions about thoughts of the positive and negative consequences of reoffending. There was little difference between the groups in the likelihood of thoughts of positive consequences: 45% of nonrecidivists said they had had such thoughts as opposed to 55% of recidivists. However, 75% of the nonrecidivists had thought about the negative consequences of acting out impulses toward criminal conduct, twice the proportion of recidivists ($X^2(1) = 11.94$, $p < .001$).

Stronger evidence on deterrence by anticipated negative consequences is contained in the answers to a direct question asking nonrecidivists what stopped them from offending. The largest proportion of answers (41%) could be categorized as fear of return to prison, while almost as many more subjects (34%) specified other negative consequences for themselves or their family. Interestingly, none said that it was the concern for possible victims that had been the primary deterrent, and only 6% said that it was the lack of positive gains from an offence. Clearly, nonrecidivist subjects felt that the negative personal consequences of reoffending outweighed the positive benefits, and this may have kept them from new offences.

Thus, one can differentiate the groups in terms of fear of negative consequences. By their own testimony, it was thoughts of the consequences that most commonly stopped nonrecidivists who had been tempted toward unlawful acts, and similar cognitions may also have prevented the others from even thinking about reoffending. This evidence only emphasizes the importance of the lack of forethought and the lack of anticipation of consequences by offenders.

Conclusion

Without question, there are major differences between our population of recidivists and the comparison sample of men who had survived for a period in the community without known reoffenses. We can see very sizeable differences in almost every area we examined, including personal background, problems experienced, coping, emotional reactions, and thoughts. Both the variety of differences and the size of some are a bit surprising when one considers that the distinction between the two groups is in some sense arbitrary. We would expect that over a longer period some of our nonrecidivists would reoffend. If an offence occurs when a person of certain characteristics meets a situation that he cannot deal with lawfully, then some men may have just been fortunate that their triggering situations had not occurred before we tested them. If we had been able to recruit a larger group, we would have attempted to predict such reoffenses longitudinally, with the expectation that those nonreoffenders who most resemble the reoffenders would have high probabilities of a later offence. Unfortunately, the numbers of nonrecidivists available in the time we had for this study obviated such analyses.

In effect, the group classification was somewhat permeable, in that some of our nonrecidivists may have been misclassified. In addition to delayed new offences, it is also possible that some of our control subjects had committed offences that were not known to authorities and that they did not admit to us. (This may help to explain why there are many more men in our nonrecidivist group who are classified as recidivists by the discriminant analysis than the reverse.) Thus, the pervasiveness and size of the differences are even more impressive than they at first appear.

It might be argued that the comparisons between groups are not justified because the groups are not well matched on background factors. To dismiss other differences on this basis would presume that the background differences determined how subjects experienced life in the community. Thus, it would be argued that whatever factors were originally responsible for their criminality were still present and still determinative of behavior and cognitions.

This seems implausible to us for several reasons. First, we find it difficult to construct a model in which distant external factors could operate so strongly on contemporaneous behavior. More important, the pattern of our results is inconsistent with any such explanation. Although some background measures showed differences that were statistically significant, this was not consistently the case, and the differences that appeared were not nearly so large as those on measures of recent emotional reactions and cognitions. The differences on historical measures are in the degree of deviance, not in its occurrence, that is, the comparison group here is not one of nonoffenders but rather of men who mostly had lengthy criminal histories but had recently desisted at least temporarily. Finally, and for some readers perhaps most convincing, the results of our analyses of covariance show that differences in current psychological measures remain after historical factors are controlled statistically. It is difficult to explain the results in terms of historical influences.

We believe that by far the best explanation is that the pattern of behavioral and cognitive differences that we have seen in this chapter is the core of a specific psychological description of the path(s) of habitual offending. The ways in which the recidivist subjects differ from other men most strongly, for example, the development of certain sorts of life problems, strong dysphoric emotional responses without self-awareness, heavy substance abuse, and actions without normal anticipation of consequences, form the basis of a description of the proximal causes of criminal offending.

When men react in these ways to life situations, they are likely to fall into criminal behavior. If they do not change, and they continue to react in ways that have in the past led them into trouble, then they condemn themselves to repeating their errors almost incessantly. It follows that those who embody these characteristics most strongly would quickly commit new offences when given the opportunity. They would also be the most consistent and persistent offenders, and over time they would have the longest criminal records. Thus, we can see how the contemporaneous differences in our groups can be used to explain the development of differences in personal history, which in effect represent the cumulative effects over time of the visible behavioral differences.

Not only can we specify the elements of the recidivist syndrome from our data, but we can use relapse theory to construct a plausible scenario for how they fit together. When one of our subjects is faced with the hassles of ordinary life, he tends to create more serious problems, for example, building minor interpersonal clashes into fractured relationships or vendettas. His coping skills are not adequate to allow any solution of his problems. He is incapable of accurately recognizing the sources of his difficulties or of finding and evaluating possible paths of action; if he does find a workable solution, his skills are too weak to successfully implement it. As a result, he becomes frustrated and depressed at his inability to achieve his desires or to improve his lot. Typically, the best way he can find to deal with his emotional distress is by use of alcohol and other drugs, making it even more difficult for him to cope well. Thus, he enters a downward spiral. At the end is a new criminal offense.

We could present several speculations on the nature of the final part of the relapse sequence, using the information presented so far. However, the question of exactly how the pattern of dynamic antecedents seen in our data leads to new offences is not yet definitively answerable. It is reasonable to assume that there are several distinct paths, each leading to different types of crimes. This hypothesis prompts us to compare antecedents across crime categories, as the central issue of the next chapter.

CHAPTER FIVE

Comparisons across Offender Groups

THE PRECEDING CHAPTERS have elucidated some aspects of the transition to recidivism, but the picture is still fragmentary. In several areas of inquiry we received information about a variety of specific events in subjects' lives and thoughts, such as the changes in specific emotional states occurring just before the new offence or the motives for a return to criminal behavior. It is possible that this shows only the variability inherent in the offence process but more likely that at least some of the variance in the overall sample comes from grouping together many sorts of offenders, with diverse current experiences and varying behavior patterns. We will argue that different sets of specific psychological events are associated with different types of current offences.

It has often been noted (for example, Gottfredson and Hirschi, 1990) that a large proportion of repeat offenders commit a variety of types of crimes. Some of the men in our sample had at some time committed all of the types of crimes according to which subjects were grouped in this study. However, the observation that these men are not specialists says nothing about whether there are unique dynamic antecedents of particular types of crimes. Rather, the latter question is best addressed by comparing the antecedents across their most recent offences, as is done here.

In terms of our understanding of the recidivism process, probably the most important question here is that of the specificity of the dynamic antecedents we have seen in the preceding chapters. For

95

example, do specific variations of deteriorating emotional health each lead to particular sorts of crimes, or do they all equally just set the stage for some sort of maladaptive outburst? In designing the study, we had anticipated this question and therefore included the selection of subjects according to three types of current offences, namely, personal assault, robbery, and other property offences. Comparisons among groups will show to what extent we can discriminate different determinative paths for these different offences, and to what extent there is a common pathway to reoffending.

To this end, statistical comparisons of the three groups were made on most measures used in the study. Comparisons were done with one-way analyses of variance for continuous variables or ordinal variables with at least three levels. For nominal or binary variables, comparisons were done with chi-squared tests. As stated earlier, some continuous variables showed badly skewed distributions, and in such cases secondary analyses were done after logarithmic transformation; however, in no case was the result substantially different than for the untransformed data, so only those values will be cited.

Personal and Criminal History

In general, background and personal history measures did not differ much across the reoffence groups. The only exception was that subjects in the Assault and Robbery groups reported more previous psychological problems than property offenders, $M = 0.8$ for the first two groups, versus 0.6 for the latter ($F(2,306) = 4.92, p < .01$); for property offenders, 47.7% had no history of such problems, as compared to 30.7% of assaulters and 37.4% of robbers.

Criminal history differentiated a bit better, in an expectable fashion. The number of prior convictions differed significantly across groups ($F(2,282) = 9.87, p < .001$), with the Property Group ($M = 32.4$) having more convictions than the other two groups ($M = 20.4$ and 20.9). The number of prior violent offences also varied across groups, with the property offenders ($M = 2.4$) having fewer than the other groups ($M = 4.2$ and 4.3; $F(2,282) = 3.83, p < .05$). Thus, there is some weak evidence of criminal specialization: Those whose new convictions involved only property had longer but less violent criminal histories.

The time to return to prison calculated from official records did not differ significantly across groups: The means ranged from 5.3 months for the Property Group to 6.2 for the Assault Group and 6.9 for the Robbery Group. At the same time, property offenders were more likely to report that they committed the (first) new offence within a month after the previous release (30.1%), with assaulters (19.1%) intermediate, and robbers (14.4%) the least likely, $X^2(2) = 7.79, p <$ .05. This ordering parallels that for the time between release and the return to prison and suggests that failure of the former measure to achieve statistical significance is the result of considerable variance. Overall, there is weak evidence that property offences occur sooner after release.

The length of the current term did differ ($F(2,306) = 15.82, p <$ .001); each group was significantly different from the others, with the longest sentences given to robbers ($M = 61.5$ months), followed by assaulters ($M = 46.5$), and the shortest terms for property offenders ($M = 30.0$). These differences indicate the current tariffs for the various types of offences because the number of current charges did not differ across groups.

Living in the Community

Measures of various behaviors and problems experienced in the immediate preoffence period are somewhat better in differentiating groups. As may be seen in Table 5.1, subjects in the Assault Group were significantly more likely to have been employed at the time of the offence, with only small differences between the other two groups. Examination of perceived problems shown in the rest of the table indicates that unemployment (or underemployment) was not in itself seen as one of the major sources of difficulties. However, the majority of subjects said that their employment situation had led to other problems; consistent with the data on rates of employment, this included a significantly smaller proportion of assaulters.

The most likely consequence that one would expect from unemployment is financial difficulty. One can see from the measures of problems experienced that money problems were cited prominently by subjects in the Robbery and Property groups, whereas this category was far down the list for assaulters. The group differences are similar

Table 5.1. *Problems experienced after release by offence groups*

Measure	Mean (s.d.) or percent		
	Assault	Robbery	Property
Employed at time of offence?	58.4	36.0	33.0[a]
Did (un)employment lead to problems?	35.0	58.0	67.6[a]
Problems mentioned at first inquiry:			
Interpersonal conflict	33.7	17.0	24.8[b]
Substance abuse	12.9	26.0	24.8[b]
Money/financial	6.9	28.0	19.3[a]
Work/school	10.9	13.0	11.9
None at all	18.8	9.0	9.2
Total number mentioned after listing and search (possible 17)	3.5	4.0	3.4
Mentioned on timeline:			
Interpersonal	55.4	30.0	30.3[a]
Substance (ab)use	28.7	42.4	29.6
Money	9.9	46.5	15.7[a]
(Un)employment	12.9	25.3	23.1
Parole or supervision	6.9	6.1	8.3
Feelings/moods	8.9	12.1	3.7
Problem seriousness ratings (0–10):			
Substance abuse	4.8	6.1	5.3
Money/financial	3.6	5.9	5.1[a]
Work/school/unemployment	3.7	4.5	4.8
Physical or emotional health	3.1	4.7	3.9[c]
Wife or family	3.4	3.5	3.4
Release supervision	3.2	2.9	4.2
Housing or living situation	2.4	3.1	2.6
Friends	2.1	2.9	2.8
Time (boredom, activities, etc.)	2.6	3.0	2.5

[a] $p < .001$
[b] $p < .05$
[c] $p < .01$

across the various types of problem measures, although robbers were much more likely to cite money problems on the timeline than the other property offenders, possibly indicating that they were more acutely or more frequently conscious of the problem.

Robbers were also most likely to cite substance abuse problems, and they were highest on every measure of this problem. In general, they seemed to regard it about as seriously as the lack of money, not surprisingly given that the two problems are linked. However, this category was clearly important for subjects in all groups, and the group comparisons are not statistically significant.

Thus, perceived difficulties with money and with substance abuse are problem areas that are associated with subsequent monetary offences, while problems in interpersonal relationships were much more important as precursors of assaultive crimes, occurring almost twice as frequently for subjects in this group as for other subjects. There was, however, no suggestion that any one group perceived a greater total of problems in the period.

Although the groups differed in the types of problems cited, there was little variation across groups in response to supervision by authorities. The only significant difference in this area was that property offenders did not feel they had gotten along with their parole officers as well as the others.

Moreover, all groups were assessed at about the same low level on each of our measures of coping effectiveness. Thus, prior to their new offences, almost all subjects were experiencing problems in living in the community but there were recognizably different sets of problems associated with offence group membership. At the same time, in none of the groups did subjects deal effectively with their problems, whatever they happened to be.

Emotions

Measures of emotional state in the preoffence period also show a consistent pattern of differences. Some of these can be seen in the frequencies of specific emotions reported for the two intervals of time surveyed, as shown in Table 5.2. Although there were no differences across groups in the combined rates of various forms of dysphoria, several specific states each differed significantly on at least one of the

Table 5.2. *Emotions in preoffence period by offence groups (percentages)*

Emotion	Previous 30 days			Previous 48 hours		
	Assault	Robbery	Property	Assault	Robbery	Property
Strong emotions experienced						
Hopelessness	20.8	22.0	10.2[a]	7.9	21.0	8.3[b]
Depression	41.6	44.0	29.6	23.8	27.0	22.2
Moody/brooding	19.8	25.0	10.2[a]	12.9	16.0	8.3
Anger	39.61	34.0	20.4[b]	39.6	23.0	20.4[b]
Frustration	40.6	39.0	39.8	27.7	28.0	36.1
Stress	28.7	28.0	25.9	19.8	19.0	20.4
Anxiety	35.6	40.0	31.5	17.8	33.0	21.3[a]
Guilt	17.8	20.0	10.2	6.9	10.0	5.6
Loneliness	27.7	20.0	20.4	19.8	11.0	13.0
Boredom	23.8	24.0	23.1	11.9	9.1	13.0
Sexual frustration	10.9	4.0	0.9[b]	9.9	2.0	0.0[b]
Nothing/numb	8.9	18.0	8.3	6.9	14.0	11.1
Positive (all)	46.5	34.0	26.9[a]	34.7	26.0	28.7
Any dysphoric[c]	81.4	81.0	77.1	69.6	66.0	67.9
Major dysphoric[d]	68.6	69.0	51.4	56.9	57.0	45.0
Strongest single emotion						
Hopelessness	3.0	3.0	3.7	0.0	10.4	2.8[b]
Depression	19.0	22.0	14.8	11.1	10.4	13.9
Moody/brooding	2.9	4.0	0.9	2.0	4.2	0.9
Anger	14.0	9.0	7.4	31.3	10.4	6.5[b]
Frustration	8.0	7.0	19.4[b]	8.1	4.2	19.4[b]
Stress	9.0	7.0	5.6	7.1	4.2	5.6
Anxiety	11.0	16.0	13.9	5.1	16.7	11.1[a]
Guilt	3.0	5.0	1.9	2.0	3.1	0.0
Loneliness	5.0	3.0	5.6	4.0	0.0	1.9
Boredom	2.0	2.0	3.7	1.0	1.0	1.9
Sexual frustration	2.0	0.0	0.0	2.0	0.0	0.0
Nothing/numb	1.0	1.0	3.7	2.0	5.2	8.3
Positive (all)	17.0	17.0	19.4	20.2	20.8	22.2
Any dysphoric[c]	77.5	78.0	76.1	69.6	62.0	63.3
Major dysphoric[d]	44.1	47.0	35.8	46.1	36.0	31.2

[a] $p < .05$

[b] $p < .01$

[c] One or more of the first 10 listed states, from hopelessness to boredom.

[d] One or more of depression, anger, or anxiety.

measurement intervals. For hopelessness, general moodiness, and anxiety, levels were highest for robbers, followed by assaulters, with property offenders the lowest. Anger also differed significantly, with the highest proportion among assaulters and the lowest among property offenders. Most reports of sexual frustration are in the Assault Group, not surprisingly since this group includes those guilty of sexual assaults. On the other hand, assaulters also were significantly more likely to report positive emotional states during the longer period.

Comparison of the two periods shows some interesting changes as the time of the offence approached. Although most frequencies decline, as would be expected in the comparison of the 30-day period to the (shorter) period of the final 48 hours, there are some notable exceptions. Most particularly, anger among assaulters does not decrease, so that it becomes strongly predominant across categories in the final preoffence period for this group. Similarly, for nonviolent property offenders, frustration does not decline as much as other states, and it predominates for them in the final period. Robbers show high levels of frustration in the final period, but also anxiety, with a considerable decline in the level of depression.

A similar pattern of results is visible in the choices of the strongest single emotional states for each period, presented in the bottom part of Table 5.2. For the longer period of a full month before the offence, only frustration shows a statistically significant difference. However, the immediate 48-hour preoffence period shows much better differentiation among the groups. Assaulters showed the most frequent anger, and the lowest levels of anxiety and hopelessness; property offenders were highest on frustration but lowest on anger; and robbers were highest on hopelessness and anxiety, but lowest on frustration.

One may construct almost the same picture by looking at the frequencies of each state within groups. For the Assault Group, the most frequent negative state was anger, with depression a very distant second. Those in the Property Group were most likely to have been frustrated, depressed, or anxious. Among the Robbery Group, the most frequent emotion was anxiety, with hopelessness, depression, and anger all tied for second rank.

Finally, one can see the same pattern of differences in emotions specified on the timeline, not shown in the table, although fewer differences are statistically significant because of generally lower rates.

The results of our standardized measures of emotional states also confirm the orderings obtained from the interview. For the Beck Depression Inventory, the mean scores ranged from 20.0 for robbers to 17.4 for property offenders to 14.0 for assaulters ($F(2,268) = 6.35$, $p < .01$). Means for anxiety scores were in the same order, from 51.2 for robbers to 49.8 for property offenders to 44.7 for assaulters ($F(2,268) = 6.29$, $p < .01$). Thus, on measures of enduring mood states, robbers appear to have the most serious problems, and assaulters seem relatively the most healthy.

The other measures lead us to expect more anger in the preoffence period among the Assault Group on our standardized anger scale. Although most of the subscales were in the expected direction, the only significant difference across groups was in the Anger Out Subscale, with the highest mean (6.4) for the Assault Group, the Robbery Group next (6.2), and the Property Group lowest (5.7) ($F(2,267) = 4.23$, $p < .05$). Given that only the one scale differs, one might interpret these results as saying that assaulters do not experience anger more strongly or more frequently, but they are more likely to follow their feelings of anger with action.

Thus, it appears that some time before the occurrence of their new offences, subjects' primary emotional states diverged in directions that are predictive of the type of new offence. Although we previously used summary measures of dysphoric states combined to show a link between dysphoria and offending, it is important to note here that it is not nonspecific dysphoria that is the precursor of offending. Rather, specific dysphoric emotions are differentially associated with each offence path. When added together, these specific states show a high rate of overall dysphoria that differentiates reoffenders from nonrecidivists, illustrating how several different parallel paths to reoffending can appear to show a single common pathway.

Thoughts

Categorizations of entries from the thoughts timeline did not show differences across groups, other than concerns with certain particular problems discussed above, such as lack of money. However, there were some differences in indices of the patterns of events and thoughts. More robbers (33.3%) were faced with a noninterpersonal coping

Table 5.3. *Subjects' perceptions of what led to offence by offence groups*

Category description	Percentage in group		
	Assault	Robbery	Property
Emotion (especially anger)	41.0	12.0	8.4[a]
Out of control	14.0	6.0	11.2
Needed money	6.0	54.0	37.4[a]
Boredom	1.0	3.0	1.9
Peer pressure	4.0	4.0	1.9
Sexual frustration	5.0	0.0	0.0
"It just happened"	20.0	6.0	17.8[b]
Other, unclassifiable	9.0	15.0	21.5[b]

[a] $p < .001$
[b] $p < .05$

challenge (most commonly inadequate money) than assaulters (17.8%) or property offenders (25.5%) ($X^2(2) = 6.16$, $p < .05$). The reverse ordering is apparent with challenges to interpersonal coping skills, seen for 26.7% of assaulters, 22.6% of property offenders, and 15.2% of robbers; the comparison between robbers and assaulters is significant, ($X^2(1) = 4.03$, $p < .05$).

There was also a difference in the pattern of events over time. Assaulters were about 50% more likely to show a uniformly low or deteriorating pattern than the other groups ($X^2(2) = 6.64$, $p < .01$). Thus, assaults may be seen as outbursts occurring after a period of negative mood states, whereas the other offence classes are better linked to conscious perceptions of (noninterpersonal) intractable problems.

This distinction is supported by evidence on subjects' perceptions of the causes of their offences, as shown in Table 5.3. The majority of robbers identified the cause as having been a need for money, but only a small minority of assaulters did so; interestingly, property offenders were intermediate. In contrast, the preponderance of assaulters said that the cause of their offences was anger, while this motivation was not very frequently mentioned by the other groups. About one in five subjects in the Assault or Property groups denied having any clear idea about the cause(s) of their offence, but this was uncommon for robbers. This and other measures together indicate that robbers are more driven by conscious motivational processes, and less likely to be following some maladaptive scenario under the predominant control of their emotions.

Alcohol and Drug Use

As we have already seen, the combined recidivist sample shows considerable evidence of substance abuse problems. When we compare across offences, it appears that each group shows high levels, but there are a variety of differences in the details of what they took and when, as summarized in Table 5.4. As a generalization, one can say that assault was preceded by the highest levels of alcohol intake, while the use of certain other drugs was differentially associated with robbery.

Some differences are visible even among measures that are not specific as to time. Robbers have the highest scores on the Drug Abuse Screening Test. On the other hand, scores on the Alcohol Dependency Scale were not different across groups, showing a substantial amount of accumulated damage over years in all groups. On intake levels for the general preoffence period, drinkers in the Assault Group tended to drink more than other subjects, and more assaulters reported a mean intake at or above a level that would likely lead to damage over time (six drinks a day). However, these differences are not statistically significant because of large variance. On the other hand, our measure of whether alcohol increased the tendency to reoffend violently did differ across groups, with the proportion twice as high among assaulters as the others.

A significantly greater proportion of robbers indulged in other drugs. When all subjects are included, the measure of days per month taking drugs showed a significant difference across groups ($F(2,304)$ = 6.34, $p < .01$), with robbers using more frequently than the others ($M = 15.0$ vs. 9.3 and 9.4). Some of the higher intake among robbers can be accounted for by differences in the use of cocaine, used by 42.0% of robbers versus 23.0% and 24.8% for the other groups ($X^2(2)$ = 10.65, $p < .01$). Overall, cannabis was the second most commonly used drug, at about 15% for all recidivists, but there was no hint of differences across groups. Opiate use also differed significantly across

Table 5.4. *Measures of alcohol and drug use by offence groups*

Measure	Assault	Robbery	Property
Mean score on ADS	8.8	8.5	7.6
Mean score on DAST	5.2	7.9	6.8[a]
General preoffence period:			
Percent using alcohol	80.0	85.0	76.1
Percent at least 6 drinks daily	32.0	23.0	24.8
FQI for drinkers	10.0	6.3	6.3
Percent alcohol increases violence	34.6	12.5	17.9[a]
Percent using other drugs	53.9	70.0	54.1[b]
Percent using daily	26.7	38.4	25.0
Mean number drugs for users	1.5	1.7	1.6
Mean days/month users take drugs	17.8	21.4	17.5
Last day (24 hrs) before offence:			
Percent using alcohol	67.0	50.5	50.9
Percent with at least 6 drinks	56.7	36.1	35.2[c]
Mean drinks for those drinking	22.5	15.3	16.9
Percent used other drugs	25.5	32.7	40.4
Mean number drugs for users	1.2	1.3	1.2

[a] $p < .01$
[b] $p < .05$
[c] $p < .001$

groups, although it was highest among property offenders (12.8%) rather than robbers (8.0%) and very infrequent for assaulters (2.0%) ($X^2(2) = 8.57, p < .05$).

Most of this pattern is duplicated for parallel measures covering the immediate preoffence period. Subjects in the Assault Group were slightly more likely to have used alcohol on the day preceding the offence. More important is the finding that when they did start they were more likely to drink to abusive levels (using six drinks as a dividing point $X^2(2) = 14.73, p < .001$; similar results are obtained with higher criteria). Overall, assaulters consumed much more alcohol daily than each of the other two groups, $M = 14.3$ versus 7.7 for robbers and 8.6 for property offenders ($F(2,298) = 5.18, p < .01$).

If alcohol use during the day before the offence was associated with assault, higher use of other drugs appeared with the contrasting types of offences. The total number of different substances used illegally on the final day was close to differentiating among the groups ($F(2,305) = 2.90, p < .06$). A similar measure, the number of consecutive days that a subject had used drugs before the day of the offence, did achieve significance, $M = 4.3$ for assaulters, 6.4 for property offenders, and 9.7 for robbers ($F(2,302) = 4.95, p < .01$).

The choice of drugs used immediately before the offence also differed across groups. For robbers, cocaine was again the most frequently used (30.0%); other offenders were significantly less likely to have used this drug (16.0% and 18.3%; $X^2(2) = 6.74, p < .05$).

The Offence Itself

Given the differences in precursors, including perceived problems and motivation, emotions, and drug use, one might also expect some differences in the offence sequence itself. For example, robbers appear to have been the most rationally motivated, many of them under financial pressure from expensive drug habits. They are thus closer to the expectations of a considered choice model than the other offenders, and one would expect that they planned their offences more and earlier. The results are consistent with such expectations.

Table 5.5 shows the amount of anticipation for the first, third, and fifth points in the offence sequence on our visual timeline, namely, the first passing thought, the first time the subject considered he might actually carry out an offence, and the first definite or detailed planning. (The other measures not in the table show exactly the same pattern.) In each case, the assault offenders show the least anticipation or planning. Even the very earliest part of the sequence did not occur more than a few minutes before the offence for three-quarters of these subjects, and few reported *any* planning. Only 6% of the Assault Group said that their total planning time was longer than 15 minutes, and we obtained about the same figure for the start of any rehearsal for the offence.

Thus, almost all of the assaultive offences were reported to be impulsive and unpremeditated. There was a minority, on the order of 10% of the assaulters, who had thought of attacking someone well in advance of their actual offence, although there was still little evidence of systematic planning. For example, this subpopulation can be seen

Table 5.5. *Selected landmarks in offence planning by offence groups*

First passing thought	Assault	Robbery	Property
A month or more	11.0	17.2	8.6
A week or more	3.0	12.1	5.7
A day or more	3.0	18.2	14.4
Hours (1–24)	4.0	12.2	8.6
Minutes (< 1 hr)	5.0	9.1	6.7
At offence	74.0	31.3	55.7
First considered	**Assault**	**Robbery**	**Property**
A month or more	3.0	5.0	3.8
A week or more	1.0	10.1	4.8
A day or more	6.0	15.2	10.6
Hours (1–24)	2.0	12.2	7.7
Minutes (< 1 hr)	6.0	11.2	6.7
At offence	82.0	46.5	66.4
First detailed planning	**Assault**	**Robbery**	**Property**
A month or more	0.0	3.1	1.0
A week or more	1.0	4.1	4.2
A day or more	5.2	12.5	8.3
Hours (1–24)	2.0	8.3	3.1
Minutes (< 1 hr)	3.1	11.5	5.2
At offence	88.6	60.4	78.3

in the answers to our question about when subjects had fantasized or daydreamed about the offence, in answer to which 7.9% said they had fantasized for several months. Visual inspection of the material on the timelines indicates that most of these exceptions were individuals who had been involved in protracted or continuing interpersonal conflict. Several subjects told us that their offences were in the nature of revenge, and these turned out to be some of the cases where prolonged prior thoughts had been noted.

In contrast to the impulsiveness of assault, the majority of subjects who committed robbery did think of their crime in advance, with less than one-third denying any prior thoughts. Although the time of advance warning was not great, we can nevertheless say that the offence was not entirely spontaneous for most of this group. The property offenders were in the middle on each measure.

The scale used to record the times given was at least ordinal, from a value of 1 for "more than one month" to 12 for "at the time of the offence." We would argue that it has the properties of an interval scale because the points of increasing temporal distance from the offence represent something like equal units in the psychological representation of time. In either case, using analyses of variance to compare groups seems easily defensible.

The results show significant differences for each of the six points. For every measure except the last (the "point of no return"), the overall differences were significant at beyond the .001 level, with Tukey Honestly Significant Difference tests showing the Robbery Group to be different from each of the others, which in turn did not differ from each other. For the final point the probability level was reduced to .05, as times converged very close to the offence, and the only significant group comparison was between the extremes of Assault and Robbery.

These results are supported and extended by the additional offence data summarized in Table 5.6. As with the timeline measures, it appears that only a minority of any group planned, rehearsed, or even daydreamed about their offences before they happened. However, there is again evidence of relatively more anticipation among robbers.

Thus, one could can say that robbery was significantly more likely to be planned or rehearsed than the other crimes, twice as likely as property offences and three times as likely as assaults. Still, only 25% of robbers said that their total planning had lasted more than 15 minutes, and only 32% said that they had done anything that could be called advance rehearsal at any time. If this seems the result of a rational process, it is only by comparison with the others, because even for the Robbery Group the amount of systematic anticipation or planning was generally minimal.

Answers from questions about the anticipation of consequences provide some final evidence on the differences between groups. While a clear majority of the monetary offenders reported having thought of positive gains from an offence, less than one-third of the assaulters did so. Interestingly, robbers and other property offenders were also more

Table 5.6. *Various offence measures by offence groups*

Measure	Assault	Robbery	Property
Never planned before offence	92.0	70.0	88.0[a]
Never rehearsed offence	91.9	68.0	87.0[b]
Never daydreamed about offence	88.1	84.0	90.8
Anything happen before first thought	81.2	86.0	87.0
Difficulties related to offence	74.3	87.9	84.3[a]
Aware something happening	37.6	69.0	62.0[b]
How handled first impulse:[a]			
Active: self-control, get help	4.0	4.0	0.0
Passive: don't resist, etc.	13.9	25.0	13.9
Act on it or plan offence	82.2	67.0	81.4
Ever think of good consequences?	29.4	71.0	59.8[b]
Material gain	10.6	58.0	49.5[b]
Peer esteem	1.2	2.0	2.8
Power	5.9	3.0	0.0
Self-esteem	0.0	0.0	0.9
Other	11.8	8.0	6.5
Ever think of bad consequences?	24.7	47.9	43.0[c]
Ever think of victim?	18.8	31.0	17.9[a]

[a] $p < .05$
[b] $p < .001$
[c] $p < .01$

likely to have thought of the possible negative consequences, although they obviously had not been sufficiently deterred. This raises the possibility that techniques to change the balance of cognitions regarding positive versus negative consequences might be an effective way to deter some types of offences.

Analyses of Covariance

It is possible that some or all of the group differences in dynamic factors are owing to the historical differences that appear. Therefore, we performed a set of analyses of covariance, much like those described in the preceding chapter. In this case we included the numbers of both previous total convictions and previous violent convictions, along with scores on the social desirability scale, as covariates before differences across groups were assessed.

The results show no visible difference in the pattern of group differences from that described in the preceding sections. Every measure that shows a statistically significant difference in the original analyses also shows significance in the analyses of covariance. Indeed, a few measures that just fail to reach significance in the former are able to cross the line with the latter, apparently because the covariates partly mask the effects.

The picture of differences across offence groups that is presented here is definitely not the result of preexisting differences in overall criminal history, nor can it easily be attributed to self-presentation biases.

Discriminant Analysis

Discriminant analyses were used to see how well the type of new offence could be classified, using the same set of 30 predictor variables as in analyses in Chapters 3 and 4. For these analyses, we shall report only the accuracy of classification and omit consideration of the details of the two discriminant functions that were generated.

The first analysis was a three-way classification using the three offender groups. The results were that correct classification was better than chance, but far from perfect. The Assault Group was identified best, with two-thirds of its subjects correctly classified. However, the figures were only 53% of the Robbery Group and 49% for the Property Group. In each case, errors were fairly evenly split between the two respective incorrect alternatives. Overall, 56% of recidivists were correctly categorized into their type of new offence.

To check whether assaulters are better identified than the others, we computed three additional analyses, each a two-way classification comparing subjects in one of the three respective offence groups against the two others combined. Assaulters were again fairly well identified: 61% were correctly classified, and only 19% of the non-assaulters were incorrectly placed with the majority of assaulters, yielding an overall accuracy of 75%. The corresponding analyses to isolate subjects in the other offence groups both yielded results in the right direction, but neither produced functions that deviated significantly from chance. Our measures of antecedents best differentiate the precursors of violent personal crimes from those of other types of offences, while they are worst at selecting out property offenders.

Conclusion

Taken together, the results in the preceding sections allow some generalizations about differences in the offence process across groups. In addition to determining the occurrence of reoffending, dynamic measures also to some extent determine the specifics of that reoffence, although the evidence is not so powerful in the latter respect as in the former. It is possible that other factors not included in the discriminant analyses are influential in the type of new offence, whether they are among the measures we gathered or not. Alternatively, it may be that the vagaries of criminal charging, combined with some indeterminacy of behavior, impose a ceiling on the level of prediction that can be achieved.

Even with the exceptions, one can see that assault was the most impulsive of the offence categories included in this study. The typical assaulter had some history of previously identified psychological problems, probably because of his history of violence, but otherwise historical factors do not differentiate him very well from other recidivists. Measures of behavior and cognitions in the preoffence period are much better able to postdict this type of offence.

Before his new offence, the typical future assaulter would have seemed emotionally healthier and better adjusted to life outside of prison than men in the other categories. He likely was managing to hold a job, and, although he did sometimes experience unpleasant emotions, he showed the least evidence of chronic depression or anxiety.

His downfall was in interpersonal conflicts, which appear as the dominant problem on every method of inquiry we used. Relationships presented him with problems that overtaxed his poor coping resources. Probably the conflicts themselves were magnified by his perceived inability to resolve them, and there was some general deterioration in both moods and cognitions. As an expression of his characteristic coping strategies of escaping or avoiding problems, he significantly increased his already high use of alcohol.

Although he became initially depressed, anxious, or frustrated at his interpersonal difficulties, at some point his emotional reactions to the problem were converted into a focus of anger. Perhaps he began to see the other person(s) in his relationships as deliberately challenging him, or perhaps the conflict infected his general outlook on the world. Perhaps also the alcohol, which initially had assuaged his anger, in larger doses exacerbated it. We have only limited definite information on what happened at this step in the process.

In any case, once the anger reached its peak the subject had become primed to an explosive point, when essentially trivial events could provide the trigger. When he was angry, a man in the Assault Group seemed to be particularly likely to convert his anger into action. When he erupted, it was almost anticlimactic: it may have been an assault on the perceived source of his problem, but often it may have appeared to be an inexplicable attack in response to a casual and trivial altercation with an almost randomly chosen victim. Whoever the target, the offence typically involved virtually no premeditation or forethought or planning. In general, assault seems to be an irrational act precipitated by emotional processes. Although there are clear precursors that may be identified by an observer, the perpetrators themselves seem to have had little awareness of their impending actions.

In contrast, robbery occurs after a very different sort of breakdown process. Its antecedents include difficulties in adjusting to life in the community, with much more evidence of general emotional malaise, such as depression and anxiety, than with assault.

However, robbery is an economic crime. Offenders who would later commit this crime had serious economic problems, such as difficulties in finding and holding employment, and they generally perceived a lack of sufficient money to support their lifestyles. This contributed to the variety of dysphoric emotions they reported, which in turn likely led to the pattern of substance abuse, including frequent use of cocaine and similar drugs to relieve depression and hopelessness, in addition to fairly high levels of drinking.

Although the pattern of change over time is not nearly so dramatic as that leading to assault, it does show some acceleration. One would expect that the heavy drug use, which starts out as a palliative for the dysphoria caused by other problems, would exacerbate financial difficulties because of its substantial cost. After a while, the drug use is as big a problem as the situation that originally precipitated it. Thus, a downward spiral ensues, which is why the offence occurs at the end of a run of drug use and increased drinking. Rather than being an emotional outburst, robbery seems to occur as a misconceived solution to a perceived major chronic problem, at the end of a self-destructive coping process that exacerbates an original smaller problem.

Although the majority of the assaulters indicated that they had not known what was happening to them, robbers were more likely to see their new criminal act as related to a particular problem, the need for money. More than the other groups of offenders, robbers had been aware that they had reached the time when they might actually commit an offence. Half had considered the possibility in advance, for a brief time that was still relatively much longer than for the other types of offences.

Some robbers had even considered the negative consequences, for example, they had stopped themselves from daydreaming about an offence because they were worried about getting into trouble, and a few had thought of the harm they might do to the victim, at least more than in the other groups. If in the end they chose robbery, it was a rational choice of a sort, although their weightings of alternatives were inaccurate and their calculations of probabilities mistaken.

In summary, robbery was a conscious solution to a particular problem. The majority of robbers had thought in advance of committing an offence, with less than one-third claiming no prior thoughts. Although these data do not seem to us to demonstrate the process of rational and considered choice that is assumed by the law, there was at least some awareness and some conscious involvement.

Our final classification, the group of nonviolent property offenders, is something of an anomaly. One can characterize assault as an unpremeditated and unplanned emotional explosion and robbery as a conscious attempt to deal with a particular problem, but it is more difficult to produce a simple image of the property offender. The offences included would seem to be the most purely economic of those surveyed, even more so than robbery, which includes elements of domination and power. Given that assault and robbery share elements of personal confrontation, so that they are both classified as violent, and given also that robbery has economic gains in common with our other property offenders, one would expect that subjects in the Property Group would be at one end of a continuum with assault at the other end and robbery in the middle.

What we found is quite different. While subjects in this group had the highest rate of unemployment on our various indicators of possible motivations, they were less likely than robbers to see a connection between their actions and their financial problems. Average values on measures that differentiated among groups were generally between the distinctly different scores for the Robbery and Assault groups.

For example, on almost every measure of anticipation, planning, or rehearsal of offences, property offenders were significantly different from the robbers and not from assaulters, so they can be said to have acted spontaneously and without much forethought, like the assaulters. At the same time, like the robbers they seem to have been motivated by the material benefits of an offence, and they saw their greatest problems as having been the combination of economic privation and substance abuse.

If offences in this group were unplanned, then one wonders how they were triggered, or at least what were their immediate antecedents. Assault is clearly directed against a particular target, and we assume that some interaction with other persons is often involved in the triggering events, but the anonymous nature of most of the offences committed by the Property Group makes it at best very difficult to place the target in a precipitating sequence.

Unfortunately, the data do not provide convincing answers to these questions. The subjects in this group were not much help themselves, with a higher percentage than in the other groups unable to give any clear statement of what they thought had led to their offences. Even if we assume that this shows only some lacunae in our set of interview questions, there is still no explanation as to why this group often resembles assaulters more than robbers.

We can envision subjects in this group falling back into illegal activities almost passively, or as the result of habit, much as chronic deteriorated alcoholics can relapse into use when they return to an environment in which they have habitually drunk to excess. Property offenders in this study had the longest criminal records of our three groups. After release from their previous term, they appear to have had the most difficulty in adjusting to life outside of prison; for example, they were bothered more than men in the other groups by supervision, and they were the most frequently unemployed. Thus, they experienced considerable frustration, accompanied by other dysphoric moods resulting from their inability to cope very well with the challenges of ordinary life.

In other circumstances they might have become channeled into the angry focus of the assault path, but, as it happened, they did not, because they had no interpersonal vector for anger or because they were not at the time predisposed to see interpersonal conflicts as personal threats. Unlike the robbers they were not energized by cocaine, and they were not as likely to be trapped by its cost, but instead they mostly chose the dulling effects of a steady intake of alcohol; those who extended their intake to other drugs were likely to choose the soporific opiates. Also unlike the robbers, they did not actively seek a solution to their current problems but preferred to avoid dealing with them and to drift, so they did not see the Big Score of the robbers as an attractive alternative.

In the end we think that they mostly fell into new offences as an unpremeditated way of dealing with their immediate needs and problems. Most likely, the "trigger" was just the appearance of an opportunity for theft or housebreaking, or an offer from friends. Given the cue value of old circumstances for old habits of long standing, this would likely suffice. We can therefore understand why subjects in this group so often had no clear attribution of how they had happened to begin reoffending.

Such a scenario is of course quite speculative, and not entirely satisfying. On the other hand, it does allow some testable predictions. For example, we would predict that habitual robbers would differ from other property offenders in the ways they attempt to solve problems, for example, that robbers would score significantly higher on a scale that measures attributions of personal control. However, nonviolent property offenders should be less likely than assaulters to (mis)perceive interpersonal hostility or to misinterpret accidental insults as deliberate confrontations.

Whatever the validity of these predictions in explaining the results of the Property Group, it is reasonable to conclude that the Robbery and Assault groups are well differentiated. Thus, we can argue that there are indeed distinct paths to various types of criminal offences. Not only are there characteristic events that distinguish recidivism generally, but there are separable antecedents to particular offences.

In making this argument, or in constructing our hypothetical scenarios for each type of offence, we are not restricted to any position on the question of chronicity or specialization across a criminal career. The antecedents of any single offence are, as we have implied in the term "dynamic," specific to a given time. Given that the offence results from an interaction between a person and his circumstances, the results may vary across a series of occurrences, such as successive releases.

To the extent that the specific antecedents are comprised of events external to the offender, the results across a series of risk periods may vary. The problems that an offender encounters after release from prison will likely differ from time to time, and thus the particular path on which he sets out will vary. If some of the specific antecedents are long-term features of the offender's environment, as we believe may be the case for a substantial proportion of nonviolent property offenders, then he will show some regularity in repeating offences of the same type, and thus there will be some degree of apparent specialization in his record of offending.

On the other hand, the things that lead a person onto one particular offence path may be internally based. In some cases the problem may be a remnant of early learning history, from deficiencies in anything from general coping strategies to molecular behavior such as money management skills. For other individuals the origins of the deviance are probably in constitutional abnormalities with substantial loadings from genetic or perinatal factors. For example, we believe that the interpersonal problems and anger that seem to be precursors of assault are probably the result of cognitive deficiencies. As such, they may be part of the syndrome that has been described for criminal psychopathy (e.g., Hare, 1991). Our identification of psychological events in the sequence leading to a single particular offence does not contradict observations that some men are destined to chronic repetition of similar sequences.

Thus, we would predict that the amount of consistency or specialization across a series of offences will be determined by the extent to which the perceived and actual situational precursors are the same. An empirical test of such an hypothesis requires a longitudinal study of individuals in greater depth than this study can provide.

Nevertheless, although it is clear that some of the pieces of the matrix are missing or uncertain, the results of this chapter provide good evidence that at least some of the details of recidivists' criminal offences are differentially associated with dynamic psychological processes. The determination of various types of actions may be somewhat chaotic, with large differences in the final result produced by miniscule differences in initial conditions, but regardless of how the results are caused we have shown that those initial conditions play an important role.

CHAPTER SIX

Comparisons within Offender Groups

WHILE THE DESIGN of the study and the selection of subjects were intended to elucidate the precursors of offending according to our trinary division of offence types, many other comparisons of interest may be done. Some of these deal with possible differences within groups, such as comparisons of subtypes of the current offence within groups. These within-group analyses can provide some additional detail on the principal direction of the study and will be presented first in this chapter. Because of the lesser numbers, our sample may not be so statistically sensitive in showing these effects, but the sample sizes are still large enough to test adequately some ideas of theoretical interest.

A great many other analyses are possible with the present dataset, including those that assess the effects of factors other than current psychological functioning. For example, we could evaluate the influence of any included historical measure on offence precursors and process. We have performed a limited set of the possible analyses, chosen because they may help to connect this study to other parts of the literature. The results form the basis of the second half of this chapter.

Among Thieves: Violent versus Nonviolent

In the preceding chapter, we considered evidence for a variety of differences associated with the type of new offence. Given that the comparisons generally neglect the specifics of previous offences, the emergence of a consistent pattern of differences in offence precursors may seem in some ways surprising. Even if career criminals are versatile in their offending, those who have committed criminal acts of certain types in the past will probably commit similar acts later. For example, those with long histories of burglary and other property offences are unlikely to have their most recent offence in the robbery category, and habitual assaulters are unlikely to turn to burglary, although they may all have offences in a variety of legal categories (cf. Chaiken and Chaiken, 1984). One would assume that there was some association between the specifics of previous records and current offences, for at least some of our subjects.

Thus, there may have been some confounding between our assignment to groups and aspects of the previous record that we have not dealt with in our previous analyses, so one could argue that the observed differences between groups are entirely the result of general and enduring characteristics of offenders. If this explanation is correct, then the differences that we attribute to the influence of specific precursors of the most recent offences would be epiphenomenal; that is, habitual patterns of criminal behavior would be the determinants of the current offence, and the differences we observe here between offence groups would be only parts of those patterns, showing at most the differences in the more distal causes of different types of criminal action.

One way to test such a possibility is to consider differences according to previous criminal history within groups. If the alternative hypothesis above is correct, then the visible antecedents of the current offence should vary according to subjects' criminal histories. For example, there should be differences between men with specialized offence careers and those with greater criminal versatility, and the differences should mirror those seen here between groups.

We chose to look most systematically at those subjects whose most recent conviction was for property offences. This group was the largest, and inspection showed that it broke down almost evenly into subgroups of those with histories consisting exclusively of property offences and those convicted previously of some violent crimes. (For this distinction, "violent" was defined as involving a personal attack or threat, that is, any form of assault, and robbery. Destructive property offences such as arson were not counted, but they were rare among this sample in any case.) Of the total of 109 subjects in the Property

Group, 49 had no prior violent offences, 27 had a single violent conviction, and 33 had two or more.

Given the differences between the group as a whole and our other groups with current offences classified as violent, the factor we wanted to test was a history of violence. For the comparisons reported here, we tested all of those with any record of violence (60) against those who had no violent record at all (49). Statistical tests of group differences were performed for every measure, both parametric and non-parametric, that might be broadly considered as dynamic: i.e., almost everything in the study except fixed historical measures.

In general, few significant effects emerged, although differences were visible in certain areas. For example, there were some indications of differences in measures of psychological well-being. Sixty-two percent of the violent subgroup reported previous psychological problems, as compared to 41% of the others ($X^2(1) = 4.70, p < .05$). The violent subgroup seemed to have had more areas of interference in their lives from alcohol use ($M = 3.3$ vs. 2.5; $F(1,107) = 5.32, p < .05$), although other measures of alcohol or drug use did not reach significance.

There is also some weak evidence of differences in behavior in the preoffence period. The violent subgroup may have been more problematic for supervision, because they reported having broken the terms of their release earlier ($F(1,107) = 4.33, p < .05$), and they rated problems with release supervisors more seriously ($F(1,107) = 6.65, p < .05$). However, on other measures the two subgroups appeared quite similar.

There is slightly more substantial evidence of differences in outlook and moods in the preoffence period, although these as well are far from overwhelming. Men with violence in their histories rated their lives in the period lower on our 100-point scale, one of the few substantial differences ($M = 52.5$ vs. 38.9; $F(1,107) = 7.55, p < .01$). There was also a difference in the strongest emotional state in the 48 hours before the new offence, with 37% of the violent subgroup specifying anger, as opposed to only 12% of those with only property offences previously ($X^2(1) = 9.53, p < .05$). The Hostility Subscale of the Multimodal Anger Inventory also shows significantly higher scores for the violent subgroup ($M = 12.1$ vs. 10.4; $F(1,107) = 5.08, p < .05$). Although these differences are consistent with the divergence in the history of violence, they are isolated, with no similar differences in other dysphoric states or, more importantly, with anger at other times.

In summary, there are some differences among offenders in our Property Group that may be associated with a previous history of violence, but they are fragmentary. Other than those mentioned above, no significant differences were visible between the two subgroups. It is unlikely that the lack of significance on other measures is owing to the loss of statistical power from reduced numbers, because the numbers within each subgroup are still large enough to show effects easily, and there was very little if any difference in the means for most important variables.

We also considered the possibility that the lack of differences results from the way we divided the larger group into subgroups. The analyses described above compare subjects with no official record of violence against those with one or more violent convictions. It might be argued that a single incidence of violence could come from unfortunate circumstances or overzealous laying of charges, so that some of those in the violent subgroup might be misclassified. Therefore, we repeated all analyses, dropping those with a single violent conviction, and used an extreme groups contrast of those with no violence compared to those with at least two previous violent convictions. The results are entirely consistent with those already presented, with no greater number of differences and no suggestion of any new effects emerging.

We must conclude that the differences between violent and nonviolent offence groups shown in the preceding chapter cannot be explained as consequences of preexisting habitual patterns of criminal behavior. When we look at the specific antecedents of recidivists' current offences, including prominently comparisons between violent and nonviolent offence types, we find distinct differences. The effects are for the most part highly significant statistically, they are consistent across similar measures, and they are spread across a variety of areas of functioning. In contrast, when we compare subjects within a current offence category according to violent or nonviolent history we find only a scattering of mostly small differences.

In short, the results of this set of within-groups analyses do not begin to replicate the between-groups effects seen in the previous chapter. Thus, we find it difficult to maintain the argument that the important differences related to the type of current offence follow from offence history. To a lesser extent, the same argument would apply to other historical factors in subjects' lives, although more definitive tests must be done with any particular measure. We believe that these results reinforce our conclusion that the results in the previous chapters demonstrate the role of contemporaneous factors in the choice of offences, and in the recidivism process generally.

This does not mean that we would deny that certain factors can give individuals enduring predispositions for particular types of crimes. Given the consistency in offending that one sometimes sees, this would be foolish. A person might acquire some habitual behaviors that put him in similar problematic circumstances time and again, or he might have temperamental or personality characteristics that are expressed repeatedly in similar maladaptive ways. In either case, he would show a pattern of repeated offending with little variation. Nevertheless, we would predict that the accompanying set of antecedent events would also repeat themselves.

On the other hand, we would predict that for a versatile offender the antecedents would vary across offences; they would be similar for each burglary for the same offender, but different from contrasting sets that occur when the person commits other offences, like robbery. Thus, proximal events are critical in determining the offence sequence, and characteristic sets of antecedents are associated with offences of various types.

This line of argument may be used to explain what happened with the subjects in the Property Group. As far as they go, the subgroup differences show some markers for the possibility of future violence in certain situations among men who had previous histories of violence, such as relatively higher scores on some measures of anger and hostility. However, the antecedent conditions leading into a nonviolent offence were also present and more consistent, and we can hypothesize that in the current case they were the more influential. Under other circumstances, the results might have been somewhat different.

Among Assaulters: Rapists versus Others

If there are differences in the precursors of different broad categories of offence, then there should also be differences associated with specific features of offences. Because it includes every sort of violent personal attacks, our Assault Group shows the most variation in the specifics of current offences of any of our defined groups. The most recent crimes for subjects within this group may include attacks that were spontaneous or premeditated, instrumentally or emotively motivated, and sexual or nonsexual in nature.

Thus, this group seemed the best suited for assessing how finely precursors can be differentiated across offence characteristics. Although some of the variation within the group is contained in information that we did not systematically have access to, such as crime scene reports, we could make some interesting comparisons within the group. Because of current public concerns with sexual assault, the analyses we chose are comparisons of rapists against other (nonsexual) assaulters.

Within the original group, the most recent offence was sexual assault on an adult female victim for 16 subjects. (Although "rape" is no longer an official offence category, having been replaced by a restructured set of charges, we shall refer to it by the more colloquial term.) As a comparison, 84 subjects from the original Assault Group were used. In order to make a clean distinction between sexual and nonsexual crimes, the two subjects with convictions for pedophilic offences were omitted from these analyses. As before, appropriate statistical tests of group differences were performed on most variables in the study. Because the statistical power of these analyses is limited by the relatively small number of rapists, we will use a more liberal criterion of reporting results than elsewhere and include nonsignificant results as noteworthy when $p < .10$.

When we consider the results, there appears to be nothing in our background or historical measures that differentiates the subgroups. However, there was a trend for rapists to survive longer than the others before rearrest on the new offence ($F(1,88) = 3.33$, $p < .08$), although there were no differences in previous criminal histories or risk measures such as the LSI. We cannot say whether this trend indicates a true difference in the time before reoffending or a difference in the speed of apprehension.

As expected, measures of offenders' lives in the preoffence period were able to differentiate better than historical factors. Rapists were less likely to have been under supervision (9 of the 16 were supervised, as compared to 67 of the 84 other assaulters; ($X^2(1) = 4.07$, $p < .05$). Only 3 of the 16 were currently married or in a common-law relationship, as compared to close to half of the others ($X^2(1) = 3.90$, $p < .05$).

The ways that subjects spent their time reflected their domestic situations. Rapists spent only about one-third the proportions of their time that the other assaulters did in family activities ($F(1,88) = 3.62$, $p < .07$), or in passive activities such as watching television ($F(1,88) = 5.30$, $p < .05$). In compensation, they spent about twice as much time in unstructured socializing with friends ($F(1,86) = 4.09$, $p < .05$).

The rapists seem to have had more difficulties living on the outside, at least in some ways. The number of problems they reported was slightly higher on each measure, although none quite reached significance. (For example, the total number of problems reported during the interview was about 10% higher.) However, every one of the rapists said that he had been worried about the direction of his life, even higher than the strong majority in the comparison set ($X^2(1) = 4.76$, $p < .05$), and almost all felt that their offences were connected to the problems they had been experiencing, as opposed to about half of the others subjects ($X^2(1) = 6.17$, $p < .05$).

There are also some weak suggestions of even more substance abuse among rapists than for the rest of the assaulters. Rapists probably began drinking sooner after release ($F(1,93) = 3.23$, $p < .08$). They also used about twice as many types of (nonalcoholic) drugs immediately before the offence ($F(1,98) = 3.94$, $p < .05$). Other measures show higher levels of alcohol and other drug intake among the rapist subgroup; although none reaches significance, we expect that there are ceiling effects on some of these measures.

At the same time, there are also indications that rapists were in some ways better adapted than other assaulters. They had lower scores on the Social Isolation Scale ($M = 3.0$ vs. 1.7; $F(1,87) = 3.42$, $p < .07$). They also had about half the assessed risk that coping responses would exacerbate problems ($F(1,81) = 4.58$, $p < .05$); although they were not more effective in alleviating problems, the reduced risk scores produced higher overall coping efficacy scores ($M = 11.3$ vs. 10.1; $F(1,81) = 6.24$, $p < .05$).

Emotional responses in the preoffence period also differ somewhat between the subgroups. For the longer 30-day period, rapists reported even higher frequencies of depression ($X^2(1) = 3.29$, $p < .07$) and anger ($X^2(1) = 4.02$, $p < .05$), than the already high frequencies among the other assaulters. Seven of the 16 rapists also reported having felt guilt, which was infrequent among the others ($X^2(1) =$

8.56, $p < .01$). At the same time, only four rapists reported sexual frustration, which was still higher than among the other assaulters where it was very infrequent ($X^2(1) = 3.81$, $p = .051$), but lower than one might have expected according to theories of rape that emphasize sexual deprivation as a cause.

Among measures of emotions in the final 48-hour preoffence period, only sexual frustration remained able to differentiate the subgroups ($X^2(1) = 9.56$, $p < .01$). However, the rate of general frustration rose among the nonsexual subgroup, so that it was significantly higher among the other assaulters than among rapists ($X^2(1) = 4.16$, $p < .05$).

The small numbers in the rapist subgroup make statistical comparisons inappropriate on the measures of the single predominant emotional state. However, visual inspection shows little suggestion of difference between the subgroups. The strongest effect visible is a conversion from other dysphoric states toward anger from the 30-day period to the immediate preoffence period, for both rapists and the others, as discussed previously.

Thus, earlier in the sequence of events rapists share the characteristic emotions that distinguish assaulters from other offenders, except that they seem more extreme, for instance, levels of anger are posssibly even higher. Sexual frustration seems to replace some of the secondary emotional states, but it was far from predominant. Only 4 of the 16 rapists cited sexual frustration as the primary determinant of their offence.

When we asked generally about determinants of the offence, relatively fewer rapists reported a connection with some particular event ($X^2(1) = 17.17$, $p < .001$). When we asked explicitly about the role of sexual thoughts in the offence, only 5 of the 16 said that they had experienced sexual arousal from anticipatory thoughts of the offence; four of these had masturbated at least once to their offence fantasies, but the other one had ignored the thoughts.

In general, the antecedents of rape seem very similar to those of other assaultive offences. At the same time, the path leading to rape is subtly different from the precursors of most other assaults. Rapists were as likely as other assaulters to hold stable jobs, but they spent their leisure differently. They spent more time in socializing and were generally not social isolates, but they did not have good current heterosexual and family relationships. These results suggest that the rapists were engaging in short-term mating strategies, as opposed to the development of stable longer-term relationships (Quinsey and Lalumiere, 1995).

In terms of the question with which we began this set of analyses, the results lead us to take a reserved position. It does appear that to some extent one can differentiate the precursors of related types of offences. Even with the reduced statistical power, there are almost twice as many significant differences in this section as in the preceding set looking at the effect of previous history, and, more important, some of the significant differences are on measures of behavior during the preoffence period.

Because of the small number of rapists in this study, and because of the lack of information on offence details, it would be unwise to adopt any strong conclusions here. However, the results of this section are consistent with our general position, and further research is warranted. In this respect, it would be especially interesting to examine features of the new offences on which we did not have information, such as the relationship of the victim to the offender or the occurrence of gratuitous violence or victim injury.

Within All Groups: Time to Offending

We have established that there are many differences in the precursors of several types of offences. However, any inferences about causation from such differences involves a speculative leap, even disregarding the retrospective nature of the data. A difference between groups implies that there is probably a link with at least one of the groups, but it is not easily attributable to any particular group. For example, if there is a difference in the amount of anger between robbers and assaulters before the new offence, does it mean that one group of men were driven to assault by anger, or that the other group were led to robbery by the lack of anger, or some combination of these explanations?

One way of dealing with this would be to compare each group separately with a control population, and to some extent we were guided in our construction of ideas about likely determinative paths for each group by visual comparisons between each offender group and our nonrecidivist controls. We are loathe to do more formal statistical comparisons of this sort because of some reservations about the appropriateness of the comparison and because of the risks inherent in proliferating redundant statistical tests.

Fortunately, the possibility of using another sort of converging evidence presents itself. Our recidivist subjects varied in the time they survived in the community before reoffending. If certain factors determine the return to criminal actions, then one might expect that in general the stronger these factors the sooner the return.

Thus, our measure of time before reoffending can be used as a rough quantifier of the strength of recidivist tendencies. Factors associated with the speed of return can be interpreted as having some role in the causal sequence. Moreover, it can be used to help confirm separate paths to recidivism and to identify the causal factors for each path. Specifically, if a factor is generally determinative, it should correlate with the time to reoffending for the entire recidivist sample and also for each group separately. In contrast, determinants linked with specific offence paths should correlate with time to reoffending within those offence groups, but not for other offences.

To this end, we calculated correlations between most of the noncategorical variables in this study and the time to reoffending. It should be noted that the size of some of these correlations is limited by the binary nature of the respective variables, such as the occurrence of particular emotional states, but we chose to calculate simple Pearson correlations for all variables for the sake of simplicity. There are also clearly limitations in the measure of time to reoffending, especially for short intervals. For example, it is affected by such things as the effectiveness of law enforcement; it may also be partly confounded with offence type, because some offences are more quickly visible or more speedily dealt with by authorities. However, we assume that such effects are not sufficient to destroy the usefulness of the measure, and mostly diminish its reliability, thus decreasing the size of the correlations obtained.

A summary of the results can be seen in Table 6.1, which includes significant correlations between the survival time and major variables. For brevity, values for some minor variables are omitted, even though a few were statistically significant; it did not appear that these had much effect on the overall picture shown in the table. Correlations with

Table 6.1. *Significant correlations with time to rearrest*

Measure	Assault	Robbery	Property
Length of criminal record	−.07	−.07	−.23[a]
Age	.19[b]	.11	−.01
Highest school grade completed	.09	.08	−.02
Age first time in trouble	.14	.04	−.18
Time of longest residence	.44[c]	.07	.05
Longest time held job	.07	.08	.06
Longest relationship	.17[b]	−.08	.15
Living in nuclear family	.08	−.08	.24[a]
LSI total score	−.32[a]	−.21[b]	−.16[b]
How soon broke release terms	.48[c]	.58[c]	.58[c]
How soon drank alcohol after release	.09	−.02	−.13
How soon took drugs after release	.21[a]	.14	.34[a]
Total drinking (FQI)	−.05	.04	.00[d]
Problem at first inquiry: work	−.10	.10	.27[a]
Problem at first inquiry: money	−.08	.14	−.03
Total number of problems	−.05	−.04	.12
Number of problems at work	.28[a]	.14	.05
Number of interpersonal problems	.07	−.05	.20[b]
Number of psychological problems	−.05	−.08	−.28[a]
Relationship with parole officer	.10	−.20	−.27[a]
Hopeless in 30 days preoffence	−.20[b]	−.01	−.08
Depressed in 30 days preoffence	−.17[b]	.07	.10
Angry in 30 days preoffence	.06	−.11	−.07
Frustrated in 30 days preoffence	−.07	−.11	.18[b]
Anxious in 30 days preoffence	−.19[b]	−.16	−.04
Beck Depression Inventory	−.12	.11	.07
State Anxiety Inventory	−.17	.12	.18[b]
Social Desirability Scale	.17[b]	.16	.07
Coping efficacy	.34[c]	.01	.31[a]
Worried life wasn't going right	−.18[b]	.03	.10
Rate life outside overall	−.20[b]	.02	.01
Confidence about success outside[e]	−.20[b]	.11	−.19[b]

[a] $p < .01$

[b] $p < .05$

[c] $p < .001$

[d] One extreme outlier is omitted.

[e] Variable scored in counterintuitive direction, so negative correlations indicate positive relationship.

offence process measures are also omitted because their meaning would be very difficult to appraise.

With the number of correlations calculated we should expect to find several that are significant by chance, so one should not take strong inferences from any single significant value. However, some interesting interpretations are suggested when one considers the pattern of significant relationships in the table.

For all groups, the time until recidivism is fairly strongly correlated with the time a subject first broke his release terms. On the surface, this appears to support supervision practices that spend much effort on monitoring violations of release terms. However, the relationship is not so direct. From inspection of a scatterplot, we can say that subjects who violated terms later were generally able to last longer without new offences, as indicated by the correlations, but many subjects violated release terms early without quick recidivism. Thus, causal attributions are difficult, and additional detail on the relationship seems necessary, probably including longitudinal data. Other than this measure, the only variable that significantly correlates with time to reoffend within each of the three groups is the score on the LSI, not surprisingly, given that it is a heterogeneous measure of risk for reoffending.

However, one can discern some patterns in the significant relationships with the time to recidivism across groups. Within the Assault Group, the speed of recidivism seems to be clearly related to the central constructs of the theorized relapse process; that is, the men who were quickest to commit new assaultive offences were those with the least stability in their previous lives; they also seemed to have the most inadequate coping ability, the poorest adaptation to life on the outside, and they tended to turn most quickly to illegal drug use. Finally, as might be expected to follow from the above, they also were more likely to experience at least one of several dysphoric emotional states over the general preoffence period. The relatively good fit to a breakdown model is consistent with results presented earlier on classification into offence groups using discriminant analysis.

Results for the Property Group also seem to implicate instability and poor adaptation, but the pattern is somewhat different. Relatively poor coping, lower confidence about success on the outside, and the use of drugs sooner after release were all associated with earlier recidivism, as for assaulters. However, for this group, dysphoric emotions in the pre-

offence period or stability of previous lifestyle make no apparent difference. Instead, some specifics of the current life situation, for example,
the subject's relationship with his parole officer or whether he was living
in a nuclear family, show associations with the survival time, and the
relevant factors from personal history are those that evidence previous
maladaptation, namely, the number of previous criminal offences or a
history of diagnosed psychological problems.

These might be interpreted as showing that relapse into a nonviolent property offence has a significant component of habituality
and may occur without obvious current motives, a picture congruent
with results shown earlier. We are also led to suggest that, if previous
experience is countered by structure and supervision in the current
life, offences of this type may be averted or delayed.

Finally, the Robbery Group shows no significant correlations with
any of the major variables other than the two in common across groups.
Earlier it was shown that a variety of factors differentiate the precursors
of robbery from those of other offences. As argued above, it may be that
the identified factors are not in the causal sequence for robbery, but
only that they differentiate it from other types of offences. Alternatively,
it may be that our measures are inadequate to reveal the temporal relationships involved. For example, the measures of perceived problems
indicate only whether a particular type of problem occurred, not when
it occurred, that is, they are insensitive to timing. If financial problems
are differentially associated with robbery, then we would expect that the
occurrence of such a problem would be followed relatively soon by a
robbery offence, but without precise information on exactly when the
problem started we can see only a differential relationship based on
occurrence or nonoccurrence, as we found earlier. Thus, the current
measure cannot appropriately be used even for the weak tests of causal-
ity possible within the present design.

While the patterns identified here for each of the offence groups
are separately not identical to those discussed in Chapter 5, there are
considerable similarities. In general, these analyses reinforce our
claims that the antecedents and determinants of different types of
offences are in fact different. They also bolster the conclusion that the
specific antecedents we have identified are at least some of the elements in separate proximal causative paths to different types of new
offences.

At the same time, it is not the case that all of our analyses show the same results. The measures that differentiated between recidivists and nonrecidivists in Chapter 4 are a superset of those that predict the speed of recidivism for all groups in the present analyses. There is some congruence in the patterns that seem to characterize each offender group, as seen both here and in Chapter 5. But the factors that differentiate among offences are not the same as those associated with recidivism in general.

The factors that are associated with the *fact* of recidivism include dynamic factors such as lifestyle, the occurrence of (some) dysphoric emotional states, and the perception of various life problems, in addition to more static measures of personal and criminal history. We would argue that these are the determinants of recidivism in a population of chronic adult offenders. In contrast, specific choices within these general categories of determinants are associated with the *type* of recidivism. For example, the particular emotion or the type of problem that occurs is differentially associated with offence categories.

The implications of this finding are very interesting. Despite some assumptions implicit in the literature, there is no reason to assume that the determinants of criminality are a fixed set that apply to all types of offences or to all offenders at every stage of their criminal careers. Rather, it is much more likely that there are several types of determinants, each coming into play for persons with different initial characteristics or at different stages in the criminal process. The ultimate aim of theory ought to be not only to identify each set of factors, but also to rationalize why and how each matters in the determinative process. We will have an adequate theory of criminal causation when we are able to understand how different individuals are separately led into criminal actions, how each learns generally to either persist or desist in his or her crimes, and how each offence is separately determined.

Risk Measures

As we have already shown, measures that are frequently used in other circumstances to index the risk of recidivism do differentiate our recidivist sample from nonrecidivists, but they are of minimal use in differentiating the types of offence within the reoffender group. This is to be expected from the reasoning above, but it could also be interpreted as the result of some problem with the validity of those risk measures.

Therefore, we decided to assess the properties of at least one risk measure within our recidivist population. This was intended as a check, but also, perhaps more importantly, as an investigation of the role of risk measures within the model developed in this study. Specifically, we looked at correlations between the Level of Supervision Inventory (LSI), a fairly good measure of current risk, and the rest of the variable set. Because of the large sample size, a great many variables were significantly correlated with the LSI score at very weak levels, and we shall neglect these. Instead, we shall generally limit discussion to correlations of the order of .30 or greater, as displayed in Table 6.2; however, the table also includes a few slightly lower correlations, for variables that are otherwise of interest.

(Separate correlations were calculated for each of the three offence groups, but in general these did not vary very much, and values across groups differed significantly in only a very few cases. Even in the exceptional cases, correlations across groups varied in size only, and they were always in the same direction. Thus, group differences were not prominent here, and only the correlations for the combined recidivist sample will be considered.)

In general, the pattern of correlations with the LSI is about what one would expect for a measure of risk. The most substantial relationships are with some indices of early onset of criminal behavior (including problems at school), with measures of drug and alcohol use, and with variables indicating adjustment problems outside of prison, especially psychological difficulties. These are neither surprising nor informative, given that the LSI incorporates such information, but there are similar – if lower – correlations between the same sorts of variables and LSI subscales that do not overlap with them.

There are also some results that are not so easily anticipated from previous findings. Among these is an association between poor coping efficacy ratings and high risk on the LSI. This reinforces previous findings that coping measures can be used to predict criminal misconduct. Even more interesting are a variety of moderate correlations with severity ratings on several sorts of problems in living outside of prison.

Table 6.2. *Significant correlations with Level of Supervision Inventory*[a]

Measure	Correlation
Time to rearrest	−.22
Total prior convictions	.25
Highest school grade completed	−.41
Number of problems at school	.26
Age first time in trouble	−.37
Longest residence time	−.20
Longest job held	−.24
Unemployed before reoffence	.43
Time after release broke terms	−.21
Frequency bored	.32
Proportion of time "hanging around"	.20
Had substance abuse problem	.43
Number of drugs used	.34
Used cocaine	.25
Frequency of drug use	.32
Feelings related to alcohol use	.32
Rating of life on outside	−.34
Confidence of success	.30
Had money problem	.36
Total number of problems	.53
Number of interpersonal problems	.28
Number of psychological problems	.46
Problem rating: work (1–10)	.30
Problem rating: time use (1–10)	.36
Problem rating: alcohol/drugs (1–10)	.38
Problem rating: money (1–10)	.28
Problem rating: friends (1–10)	.25
Problem rating: health (1–10)	.32
Hopeless in 30 days preoffence	.31
Depressed	.21
Frustrated in 30 days preoffence	.23
Anxious in 30 days preoffence	.24
Any dysphoric state 30 days preoffence	.33
Positive feelings 30 days preoffence	−.26
Deteriorating emotional tone preoffence	.23
Beck Depression Inventory	.42
State Anxiety Inventory	.28
Alcohol Dependency Scale	.40

Table 6.2. *(cont.)*

Measure	Correlation
Drug Abuse Screening Test	.45
Anger Inventory: Anger Arousal	.31
Anger Inventory: Anger In	.30
Time Use and Time Planning Scale	−.25
Social Desirability Scale	−.40
Coping efficacy	−.27
Coping adequacy	−.56

[a] All values significant $p < .001$.

When we look at the interaction of coping efficacy and problems, as operationalized in the measure of coping adequacy, the correlation becomes fairly substantial. Finally, the LSI correlates with a variety of mood states in the preoffence period. These results indicate a relationship between assessed risk, at least as measured by the LSI, and specific antecedent conditions to offending.

If we assume that these correlations can be replicated with other risk measures, it becomes necessary to consider why such relationships exist. We believe that an answer can be found in the way(s) that actuarial scales obtain their predictive ability. One may conceive of an instrument for assessing risk such as the LSI (or comparable instruments) as an abstract measure of tendencies toward criminal behavior. However, such an intangible construct is difficult to comprehend in any concrete way. A better understanding can come through an analysis of the scale elements and how they might function.

Even though they have almost always been chosen by some actuarial method, the variables that have been used in classical risk prediction scales can probably all be classified into three groups. The first type consists of historical measures of personal behavior that indicate the degree to which criminal patterns of behavior have been present in an individual's past and thus may be regarded as habitual. Measures of criminal record are of course prominent in this group, but lifestyle measures such as the longest residence at a single address also indicate the degree to which patterns of living that are associated with criminal behavior have characterized an offender's life. Given the considerable

persistence of behavior over time, it can be expected that past misconduct will continue into the future, so such measures work as valid
predictors of recidivism. When they are incorporated into actuarial
scales, they predict future criminal actions because they capitalize on
the consistency of behavior over time.

A second type of variable commonly chosen for predictive scales
consists of indices of conditions or behaviors, primarily early in life,
that are known or presumed to be predictors, or even determinants,
of persistent future misconduct. Early onset of criminal behavior, or
dropping out of school, are often chosen, although there are other
similar measures not commonly included in actuarial scales for various reasons, such as perinatal complications. We would argue that
variables in this category are predictive because they are historical
determinants of some of the behavioral patterns associated with
offending, or at least that they are closely related to significant
determinants of those behaviors. For example, the occurrence of
early classroom aggression makes it more likely (although far from
inevitable) that a boy will cope with interpersonal situations aggres-
sively later in his life. Information that some of the determinants of a
pattern were historically present does allow one to predict the pres-
ence of that pattern in adult life. However, the linkage is quite
indirect and imperfect.

Finally, the third type of measure assesses a subset of the more
general and stable antecedents of recidivism more directly. For example, this group includes scores for a history of substance abuse or
criminal associates. It can be seen that these measures are components of the ways that individuals perceive and deal with situations and
people in their lives, and our data confirm those of many other
investigators in showing their importance in offending. Thus, one
would expect to see correlations of at least moderate size between
scales that include them and direct measures of other behavioral
patterns that lead to recidivism.

Thus, at least some of the measures used in actuarial scales have
domains that overlap with the model we have been describing. The
second and third classes described above are useful because of direct
or indirect relationships with some of the behavioral antecedents of
recidivism, while those in the first class capture the habituality of
offending. When the three types of variables are combined into a

single predictive scale, there are substantial correlations with many of the antecedents that are central measures in this study, as one can see in Table 6.2.

Indeed, it would be surprising and problematic if there were no relationship between a conventional risk assessment scale and those measures. In effect, we have argued that the dynamic psychological antecedents of recidivism, including both large-scale and relatively persistent patterns and labile local processes, are the site of action of the recidivism process. Therefore, measures of the antecedents should by themselves work as predictors of risk, and at least some of them must almost necessarily be correlated with other valid predictors of risk.

We are led by this reasoning to an interesting possibility. The focus of study here has been on certain ways of reacting, cognitively, affectively, and behaviorally, in ordinary life situations. If we are correct, then current risk prediction instruments derive their empirical effectiveness from indirectly measuring some of the critical elements in the process. Measuring the occurrence of these specific antecedents more directly provides an alternative way of assessing the probability of a new offence that might have some advantages over classical actuarial scales.

As we have discussed earlier, current risk prediction instruments have generally neglected the dynamic nature of the recidivism process, and this limits their ability to predict correctly in some cases. In particular, the occurrence of change within an individual violates the assumptions of continuity inherent in most scales, and it provides a source of significant inaccuracy. Even the persistent and pervasive patterns of interactions with the environment that we have described are only relatively static, because they can be – and often are – changed or modified. For example, after an effective rehabilitation program current behaviors will change, but static risk assessment will not; in such a case, the correlations between psychological antecedents and actuarial risk scores will be reduced, and direct dynamic measurement will be a more accurate method of prediction than classical actuarial instruments.

The final chapter will elaborate on the possibility of predictive techniques based on the model we have developed here, along with some other implications of this research.

CHAPTER SEVEN

Final Considerations

IN EACH of the preceding chapters we have considered implications of our data in context, and it would be redundant to repeat or even review that discussion here. However, there are some general issues raised by the results as a whole. This chapter is largely comprised of examination of some of the wider implications of the research reported here.

In particular, we will survey the consequences of our data in three general substantive areas. First, the results affect our theoretical understanding of the causes and maintenance of criminal behavior. Second, they also have significant implications for policies and practices in the supervision of released offenders. Finally, they hold promise for new directions in the development of instruments and procedures for predicting recidivism.

However, before discussion of those general issues, a brief reconsideration of methodological issues seems appropriate because any conclusions depend on how well one is convinced of the validity of the data. This study has demonstrated what appear to be strong links among poor coping skills, dysphoric emotional states, certain perceptions and cognitions, and criminal recidivism. Before we can consider causation (or its practical consequences) we must reexamine the nature of our information on the period before reoffending.

Any reservations we have about according causal status to the variables measuring preoffence behavior involve the methodological limitations of the study itself. These limitations include (1) the threats to validity posed by faulty or biased recall of past events and the difficulty of establishing temporal relationships, (2) the reliance on self-report and the attendant possibility that subjects lied about what had occurred or were simply unaware of what was actually happening to them, and (3) the small number of nonrecidivist comparison subjects and the absence of a noncriminal control group, which raises the issue of the specificity of the effects found.

These issues can be addressed partly with information obtained in the study itself and partly by using information from related research. Turning first to the problems posed by the retrospective nature of the study, we recognize that subjects' recall may have been colored or filtered in the light of subsequent events before we encountered them, or otherwise distorted by cognitive needs for coherence or protection of the self or self-image.

However, it is important to consider the types of variables that were included in the study and how they were measured. For example, the measures of coping skills, although obtained after the events in question, are measures of capacity and not easily subject to distortions of recall. Moreover, this measure is known to be related to the likelihood of recidivism in prospective research (Porporino, Zamble et al. 1990). Similarly, although dysphoric mood is subject to biased recall, related research indicates that it precedes offending: Staff descriptions of dysphoric mood have been found to be related to subsequent eloping and/or reoffending among supervised mentally disordered offenders (Quinsey et al., in press). Thus, although some variables may be susceptible to recall biases, the majority of the important measures are probably not, and even when distortions are possible, the validity of the measures can be established elsewhere.

The issue of the extent to which subjects lied or were unaware of critical events pertains primarily to comparisons of the nonrecidivists with the reoffenders. It is unlikely that the recidivist subjects as a whole were differentially motivated to exculpate themselves, and even less likely that they would be differentially aware of their life circumstances. Although the differences found between the recidivists and nonrecidivists could be accounted for by differential motivation to be truthful, this explanation is fatally undermined by the results of the previously mentioned prospective studies. In any case, the meaning or purpose of many of the measures used is far from obvious, subjects had little information about the theoretical approach of the investigators, and it is extremely unlikely that a person with motivation to deceive could have divined how to answer questions in a way that would produce the obtained results.

The small number of nonrecidivist subjects and the absence of a nonoffender control group raise questions about the stability and representativeness of the comparison between recidivists and non-recidivist groups. These difficulties can be addressed in several ways. First, many of the psychometric instruments that were employed (e.g., the Beck Depression Inventory, the MAST, and the DAST) have norms derived from a variety of nonoffender samples. These norms show that the nonrecidivists scored much closer to nonoffender samples than to the recidivists. Similarly, the LSI has been used on large numbers of offenders, and the scores for the nonrecidivist subjects on this instrument indicate lower risk than for the recidivists.

These arguments all lead us to conclude that the principal findings are defensible and very likely correct. Moreover, the reservations we consider here had been largely anticipated in our planning. Not only can they be dealt with by arguments based on specific features of our data (or others'), but even stronger counterarguments can be found when one considers together the complete pattern of our results.

For example, one may consider discounting the differences between recidivists and nonrecidivists for reasons cited above, but none of the problems raised here can account for the differences across offender groups. Moreover, there was very strong consistency among the deliberately redundant set of measures we had included, which makes it difficult to dismiss any given set of answers as an artifact of the method of questioning or of cueing recall. Finally, statistical controls show that social desirability (at least as measured by the common instrument we used) has no substantial impact on either the differences between recidivists and nonrecidivists or those among offender groups.

On the whole, then, we believe that the results of this study are substantially valid. Although the methodology imposes some limits to interpretation, this is no more the case here than in any other single study. While we wish to maintain a relatively cautious stance until the results have been replicated by other methods and extended, we do maintain that the findings here are a substantive addition to our knowledge of what occurs in the process of criminal recidivism. Thus, consideration of the consequences in several directions is warranted – or perhaps even required.

Theory

At one end of the spectrum of concreteness are the implications of our data for theory. As we stated at the outset, our ultimate goal is a general understanding of criminal behavior that fits within rigorous contemporary scientific psychological theory, and the explanation of recidivism would be one part of this general perspective. The information that we have obtained here gives us some insight into the latter and more specific part of the long-term objective, although we are obviously still far from the more general goal.

Although we cannot provide a detailed model for the evocation of criminal actions at this time, from our data we can outline what appear to be the principal types of elements in the recidivism process, as in the first attempt of a model illustrated in Figure 7.1. We will not defend strongly all of the links shown between parts of the model, and it is possible that we will need to add more interactions and feedback loops between the various stages, but from the current data it does seem clear to us that there are separate roles for each of the components represented. Some readers will perceive the debt this model owes to the now classic description of the coping process proposed by Lazarus and Folkman (1983), but it has been considerably adapted to criminal actions, and especially to fit the data presented earlier.

A person is often confronted with potentially problematic situations to which he or she must react. Such situations are generally external in origin, and they are not only dynamic but often labile, appearing quickly and rather unpredictably. When a challenging situation does occur, it leads to the sort of processes usually subsumed under the rubric of coping behavior. We have seen that certain types of problems are particularly problematic for chronic criminal offenders.

Probably the first things that happen are emotional and cognitive reactions to the occurrence of the precipitating situation. The person

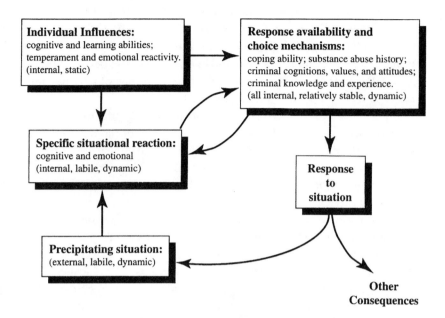

Figure 7.1. A tentative model for the criminal recidivism process.

must appraise the situation and decide what consequences it might have. For example, it might be judged to be personally threatening; at least in persistent criminal offenders, this would likely produce an emotional response involving anger. Like the precipitating situation(s), the initial cognitions and affect changes are capable of changing quickly, that is, they are dynamic and labile. However, they are also strongly influenced by individual ways of perceiving and reacting to events, what we usually refer to as personality or temperament. We see the latter as biasing or directing a person's reactions to situations in certain directions. Although it is possible that temperament could be changed with concerted effort, there is no convincing evidence of such change in the literature, so it should be considered as static.

In the present data, there is evidence that both static and dynamic emotional reactions need to be considered in explaining recidivism. For example, many of the habitual offenders in our sample showed evidence of relatively long-term propensities toward depression, with a history of such disturbances and in their scores on standardized questionnaires, but there are also consistent indications of a progression of transient dysphoric affective reactions before the occurrence of new offences. Although we did not measure cognitions with anything close to the same level of detail in this study, we expect that there are similar influences from both static long-term ways of reacting and labile short-term perceptions or appraisals.

A person's cognitive and affective state constantly inform the mechanisms used to select and guide actions. After the initial reaction to a situation, the elements of response availability and choice mechanisms come into play. Among these are the ways that a person has learned to deal with situations effectively, usually characterized as coping ability, but the existence of practiced or even habitual types of maladaptive behavior is also important. The choice of actions depends on cognitive evaluations about what would be effective or personally appropriate and thus subsumes attitudes, self-image, and values, as well as other mechanisms. It also depends on the availability of behaviors in a person's repertoire and their accessibility to conscious memory.

While the mechanisms of action choice are structural, the set of responses from which choices are made is strongly affected by individual learning history, so the effective choices are capable of change. Therefore, measures related to response availability or selection should be classed as dynamic, even though effecting desirable change is sometimes difficult. In the data from this and other studies, one can see many influences of response factors, including the strong effects of habitual substance abuse, prior criminal experience, criminal associates and patterns of socialization, and other indices of prior experience or habits.

Because we have dealt here only with persistent serious adult offenders, both the figure and our description of components in the model ignore questions about the origin of criminal behavior that would be critical with other groups, such as first-time or juvenile offenders. To achieve a comprehensive description of criminal actions, the approach represented here must be extended to include the original causes of the more stable elements in the model, specifically, temperament and response mechanisms.

The determinants of the two are probably quite different. As we conceive of it, temperament is formed relatively early, with heavy genetic and perinatal loadings, and environmental influence only in infancy and the preschool years. On the other hand, response learning can occur throughout life, and there are clear environmental effects visible at many stages. Available evidence shows the predominant importance of parenting in preschool and early school years; later, as a child's world widens, school and other extrafamilial factors become more important; by adolescence, the wider social environment provides the most influential factors, like identification and rejection of deviant individuals by noncriminal peers, and acceptance by criminal peers and associates.

To deal with the longitudinal development of criminal behavior, or with broader populations of offenders, we would need to formally incorporate these findings into our model. This could be done with some help from previous classic work, such as that of the Gluecks (1959) or the Cambridge longitudinal study (West and Farrington, 1973; Farrington, 1995), or insightful meta-analyses such as those of Loeber and Stouthamer-Loeber (1986). However, we have chosen not to do so now because we feel that it may be premature, and because we desire to emphasize the distinctive role of contemporaneous factors and to concentrate on recidivism. We believe that the research reported here represents a step toward a workable psychological representation of recidivism. If it is incomplete, it nevertheless does show that the present approach can lead to information about criminal acts that goes beyond what was known before, and we believe it shows that our eventual goal is a plausible one.

Within the limits of its design, the study contains several sorts of interesting new findings. It does appear that for many released offenders a definable series of emotional and cognitive events occurs antecedent to new offences. Moreover, it is also clear that there is not a single determinative path: Events vary somewhat across the type of new offence, and perhaps also along other dimensions, such as certain dispositional characteristics that differentiate offenders or major features of their postrelease environments.

The proportion of offenders for whom the event sequence(s) have been – or even could be – well described is still uncertain. We also do not know how much uniformity there is among the sequences of anticipatory events, even within classes of offences, or what are the parameters of individual variation. However, there is probably enough uniformity that an objective observer could in many cases correctly anticipate an impending offence. Several aspects of the results indicate that this might be done most successfully in cases of violent personal attacks, the class of events where accurate prediction would be most socially useful.

Thus, although many of the details must still be provided, the results we have obtained show the usefulness and the potential power of viewing recidivism as the result of a dynamic psychological process. Not only is this approach an alternative to the search for static correlates that has characterized past research, but it offers an explanation as to why static and historical variables are able to predict future recidivism, as outlined in the preceding chapter. The present model offers a more comprehensive and parsimonious alternative to older explanations based solely on static historical measures.

Our argument implies that the ability of historical factors to predict recidivism will be imperfect, as is of course the case, but, more important, it indicates where and why the inaccuracy will originate. Although established sequences may be strongly determinative of continuing criminality in repeat offenders, there are many ways for a break in the pattern to occur. There may be changes in the external environmental antecedents of offending. There may be maturational development of individual offenders (cf. Zamble, 1992; Shover, 1996). Or there may be altered ways of perceiving, coping, or interpreting events and conditions, perhaps as the result of rehabilitation programs that target such behavior. Each of these types of events would violate the assumptions of continuity inherent in static measures and likely lead them to generate invalid predictions as a result. In contrast, changes can be incorporated easily into a conceptualization that includes the ongoing role of dynamic factors, and measured practically by repeated surveys of behavior after release to the community.

From this, we are led to a more general point about the diversity of factors antecedent to offending, both across offence types, as we have shown before, and across stages of criminal careers. The original causes of the first appearance of any sort of behavior are not the same as the determinants of its maintenance. For example, people begin smoking largely because of social pressure and image manipulation, but maintenance is clearly an addictive process. Similarly, in the case of criminal behavior, factors in the social environment seem influential as determinants of initial delinquency for a substantial proportion of offenders, as previous investigators have found, but habitual offending is better predicted by looking at an individual's acquired ways of reacting to common situations. That is, the proximal antecedents (and thus also the most accurate predictors) of reoffending should be somewhat different for repeat offenders than for novice or inexperienced criminals. This has practical implications for the prediction of recidivism, as well as theoretical import.

Finally, while we are considering the theoretical implications of our data, we ought to evaluate in retrospect the theoretical model with which we began this research. In general, the combined coping-relapse model seems to survive quite well. It is generally quite consistent with our a posteriori model, and it was very useful in directing the strategy of investigation. However, there are ways in which the process revealed here differs from that described most commonly in addictive relapse. The relapse model fits the case of assaultive offences most closely, but other types of crimes do not seem to conform as well. For example, the role of emotional mediators does not seem to be as important for robbery offences as for personal assault. Thus, we can sketch several different offence paths, each with a different set of typical antecedent events and a different type of result. This differs from the single determinative path in the relapse model.

There is also an important external difference between addictive relapse and criminal recidivism, because the first slip in the case of criminal behavior has serious potential consequences, and therefore the cognitive processes dealing with initial violations of abstinence described in the case of addictive relapse are of less relevance here. Unfortunately, this probably means that the techniques that will be effective for the avoidance of relapse into criminality are more circumscribed than those with substance abuse. Moreover, the evidence indicates a very rapid unfolding of the breakdown process in some cases, and this argues that preventive efforts must concentrate on the recognition of the earliest signs of susceptibility in order to avoid the rest of the sequence. Thus, the results of this study help to delineate what may be the most successful course for preventive actions, but the difficulties are apparent as well.

Practice

After the abstractions of theoretical constructs, it may be appropriate to consider next the most concrete consequences of our results for application. The results regarding the effectiveness of supervision practices are sobering. The majority of subjects reported having had few problems with their release supervisors, but at the same time they appraised supervision as having had little effect on their behavior. Their judgments are supported by indices of that behavior: There appears to have been almost universal violation of restrictions imposed in the terms of release, usually very soon after release.

There is both good and bad news in these findings. Recurrence of offending was not nearly so quick as violations, so one may take hope in the finding that violations such as drinking under a prohibition are not serious indications of impending recidivism. The amount of drinking or drug use and the way they fit into the pattern of other behavior are more important than just the failure to maintain abstinence. Still, the most prominent specific task of release supervisors is to monitor and enforce compliance with the conditions of release, and the results indicate that this task is not being performed effectively.

One does not know whether a group of unsupervised releasees would be even worse, so we cannot say that the present system fails entirely to act as a brake on the appearance of new offences. However, we must conclude that current levels or types of supervision are almost totally ineffective in controlling the behavior of releasees, despite the best efforts of release supervisors. While this is damning, it is very much consistent with all of the relevant data in this study, and with our conclusions regarding the process of events in recidivism.

Much of the problem rests in the assumptions implicit in the tasks chosen for supervision. On the basis of evidence that certain events are frequently associated with recidivism, it has become commonplace to monitor events like use of intoxicants as a tactic for preventing new crimes. Unfortunately, the associations in question reflect only a small part of the sequence of events that precipitate recidivism. Using them to direct action such as revocation of release is akin to using a person's coughing to diagnose a recurrence of tuberculosis. Even "intensive supervision" programs usually consist of more of the same, and their lack of success (Genfreau, Cullen, and Bonta, 1994) is hardly surprising.

Supervision might become more effective in reducing recidivism if it were to focus on some of the mundane events in offenders' lives, especially the problems they encounter, how they manage those problems, and their moods or emotional reactions. If these were regularly monitored, then the specific antecedents of various types of new offences could be observed and used to direct preventive action. Periodic monitoring would allow charting of changes in moods or global cognitions, especially signs of deterioration. In effect, supervision would become a monitoring of the psychological thermometer of individuals after release.

We must stress that any such effort must be done preventively to catch the signs of impending offences well in advance. Many offences, especially violent personal assaults, are triggered easily with the event sequence unfolding very rapidly; once a critical point has been reached, it would be virtually impossible to intervene.

Thus, in effect, we are recommending that the role of supervision shift away from the relatively passive task of monitoring violations. Instead, it should adopt the more active tasks of monitoring early elements in the psychological and behavioral sequence of preoffence events, and execute or at least direct intervention when a need is indicated.

Such monitoring and intervention might be seen as the sort of intrusive oversight of which social welfare systems have sometimes been accused. However, although it might be inappropriate in other circumstances, it is justified in the case of serious criminal offences, both as a form of protection for society and as a didactic system for helping released offenders to avoid returning to prison. We deal with financial bankruptcy by the appointment of trustees to oversee transactions. Other transgressions might best be treated analogously, with a person who is likely to commit criminal offences taken under moral receivership for a period, until he demonstrates the capability of managing his own affairs without the likelihood of further infractions.

Of course, this can be justified only if we are correct that such a system is both practically feasible and demonstrably effective in reducing recidivism. Although this remains to be definitively established, we believe that there is already sufficient evidence to motivate the development of experimental programs in which current practices for the supervision of released offenders are substantially altered.

Prediction

Having considered first the theoretical import of this study, and then some of its empirical implications for application, we turn now to the most important intersection of theory and application, namely, the prediction of future criminal offences. We shall argue that the results of the present study have an important potential role in the future development of predictive techniques.

At the very least, our results suggest that one ought to include measures of current psychological state in predictive scales, using them to supplement static predictors. To do so would sample from a wider universe of meaningful predictor variables, which alone ought to produce an increase in predictive power. This will be especially the case if we are correct in our hypothesis that many of the variables in actuarial scales work as predictors because they indirectly measure either temperament or the less labile but still dynamic ways of thinking or behaving that are central in generating renewed criminal behavior: Direct measures are better than indirect. Such an extension of the set of predictors would almost certainly allow an increase in the accuracy of predictions and in identifying individuals who present a high risk over long periods.

Second, we would be able to measure the dynamic elements in a truly dynamic fashion, by repeating the measurement process periodically while monitoring behavior after release. Like most other significant behaviors, recidivism is the result of the continuous interaction between behavior propensities and the environment. The risk of a new offence is a dynamic product of this interaction, so, as both the person and his environment evolve over time, the risk of recidivism can also change continuously.

Measurement at a single time, no matter how well executed, cannot allow for subsequent events and changes. In contrast, a scale that incorporates remeasurements gives us the possibility of updating predictions periodically. For example, the effects of ongoing rehabilitation programs in lowering risk could be included in subsequent assessments. Periodic remeasurement is especially important for the more labile elements, such as the exacerbation of risk produced by newly developing environmental situations. If included as part of a supervision process with the task of monitoring short-term dynamic risks, as proposed earlier in this chapter, periodic remeasurements could result in a level of advance warning of recidivism far beyond what is possible with a single determination of risk. If such monitoring and remeasurement prove too expensive to be used in all cases, they could at least be used for high-risk offenders.

Dynamic updating could be combined with statistical techniques such as survival analysis to yield predictions of risk and how it changes over time. The resultant functions would likely have greatest accuracy for the immediate future and diminishing accuracy the farther one goes from the time of prediction. Remeasurement of the most labile measures in the prediction equation would serve to reset and update the curve. (One could make an analogy here to contemporary meteorological forecasts, which are quite accurate in the short term but decreasingly so over time as chaotic processes evolve.)

Thus, scales that feature a combination of both historical and current psychological measures would likely increase the accuracy of predictions beyond what is currently possible, and they would also have the possibility of further gains with the inclusion of longitudinal follow-ups. Such scales would also avoid most of the other problems with actuarial scales based solely on static measures, as presented in Chapter 1.

However, we might go even farther in the predictive use of relevant psychological antecedents of recidivism and employ them as replacements for static historical variables rather than merely as supplements. Instead of just adding the sorts of measures we have been considering here to the prediction model, one could allow them to assume most – or even all – of the predictive load carried by static variables in previous scales. Again, if static measures can assess the propensity of reoffending because they are indirect indications of psychological states, or because they assess the habituality of offending, they could be functionally replaced by more direct and current measures of the processes actually active in recidivism. Thus, it is possible that, once one includes a set of dynamic and psychologically meaningful measures in predictive instruments, historical or static measures will not in themselves provide any useful additions to predictive power.

We would not go even farther and argue that it will be possible or desirable to adopt a scale composed entirely of dynamic components, because, as discussed earlier in this chapter, some static aspects of personality are probably important parts of the determinative sequence. Psychopathy is probably a case in point.

However, we could and should aim at constructing a predictive scale based entirely on an analysis of the psychological antecedents of recidivism. Among these, the predictive ability of the different types of dynamic elements depends somewhat on the length of time under consideration, with the relatively stable response-selection mechanisms the best predictors over longer periods and the more labile measures critical for short-term prediction, especially when they are measured repeatedly to assess changes. We expect that an optimal scale will contain a combination of measures of each type. For example, it might include measures of psychopathy and coping ability, as well as the occurrence of particular problem situations and emotional states. We have a strong expectation that we can derive a scale of this type that will predict reoffending significantly better than current actuarial scales.

The possibility of predictive instruments based on the explanation of the criminal process that has been presented here, or on other similar theories, is desirable for other reasons as well. There is often resistance to current actuarial scales because of perceptions that they are "mechanical" in nature, but a scale whose components represent elements of a explicit and understandable model of behavior would be more likely to be accepted as an alternative to clinical judgments. Thus, not only would it be more often correct, but it would also be more likely to be actually adopted and used by decision makers.

In summary, we believe that the sort of information we have found in this study can be used quite practically to improve our prediction of recidivism. Whether we use current and dynamic measures to supplement static factors or to supplant them, predictions based entirely or partly on a psychological model of the recidivism process could become substantially more accurate than those currently available. Of course, these expectations remain to be tested.

Obviously, this would require a protracted and substantial research effort. As we see it, such an effort should begin with some small-scale studies aimed at developing simple and reliable field measures for the factors that appear to be of importance, proceed to studies of intermediate size in which different combinations of the various measures are developed and tested for their ability to collectively predict recidivism, and culminate in a large-scale prospective validation of the predictive usefulness of the resultant comprehensive model. Ideally, at the end we should be capable of predicting the risk of every individual offender committing each of several types of offences, and how those risks change over time.

Although the investment is considerable, the potential value of the results is even more sizeable. Without it, the promise demonstrated in the present work will not have been realized. We believe that it is well worth doing.

References

Adams, K. (1983). Former mental patients in a prison and parole system: A study of socially disruptive behavior. *Criminal Justice and Behavior, 10*, 358–84.

Andrews, D.A., and Bonta, J. (1994). *The psychology of criminal conduct.* Cincinnati: Anderson Publishing.

Andrews, D.A., and Friesen, W. (1987). Assessments of anticriminal plans and the prediction of criminal futures: A research note. *Criminal Justice and Behavior, 14*, 33–7.

Andrews, D.A., Kiessling, J.J., and Kominos, S. (1983). *The Level of Supervision Inventory (LSI-6): Interview and scoring guide.* Toronto: Ontario Ministry of Correctional Services.

Andrews, D.A., Kiessling, J.J., Mickus, S., and Robinson, D. (1986a). The construct validity of interview-based risk assessment in corrections. *Canadian Journal of Behavioural Science, 18*, 460–71.

Andrews, D.A., Kiessling, J.J., Robinson, D., and Mickus, S. (1986b). The risk principle of case classification: An outcome evaluation with young adult probationers. *Canadian Journal of Criminology, 28*, 377–84.

Annis, H.M., and Davis, C.S. (1989). Relapse prevention. In R.K. Hester and W.R. Miller (Eds.), *Handbook of alcoholism treatment approaches* (pp. 170–82). New York: Pergamon Press.

Baird, S.C. (1981). Probation and parole classification: The Wisconsin model. *Corrections Today, 43*, 36–41.

Barton, R.R., and Turnbull, B.W. (1979). Evaluation of recidivism data: Use of failure rate regression models. *Evaluation Quarterly, 3*, 629–41.

Beck, A.J., and Shipley, B.E. (1987). *Recidivism of young parolees. Bureau of Justice Statistics Special Report.* Washington, D.C.: U.S. Department of Justice, Bureau of Justice Statistics.

Beck, A.T. (1967). *Depression: Clinical, experimental and theoretical aspects.* New York: Harper and Row.

Blackburn, R. (1993). *The psychology of criminal conduct: Theory, research and practice.* Chichester, England: John Wiley.

Bonta, J., and Motiuk, L. (1985). Utilization of an interview-based classification instrument: A study of correctional halfway houses. *Criminal Justice and Behavior, 12,* 333–52.

Bonta, J., and Motiuk, L.L. (1987). The diversion of incarcerated offenders to correctional halfway houses. *Journal of Research in Crime and Delinquency, 24,* 302–23.

Bonta, J., and Motiuk, L.L. (1990). Classification to halfway houses: A quasi-experimental evaluation. *Criminology, 28,* 497–506.

Brown, R.C., D'Agostino, C.A., and Craddick, R.A. (1978). Prediction of parole outcome based on discriminant function. *Corrective and Social Psychiatry and Journal of Behavior Technology, Methods and Therapy, 24,* 93–101.

Burgess, E.M. (1925). *The working of the indeterminate sentence law and the Parole System in Illinois.* Springfield, Ill.: Illinois Parole Board.

Carlson, K.A. (1973). Some characteristics of recidivists in an Ontario institution for adult male first incarcerates. *Canadian Journal of Criminology and Corrections, 15,* 1–15.

Chaiken, M.R., and Chaiken, J.M. (1984). Offender types and public policy. *Crime and Delinquency, 30,* 195–226.

Farrington, D.P. (1995). The development of offending and antisocial behaviour from childhood: Key findings from the Cambridge Study in Delinquent Development. *Journal of Child Psychology and Psychiatry, 360,* 929–64.

Fischer, D.R. (1981). *The use of actuarial methods in early release screening.* Statistical Analysis Center, Office for Planning and Programming, State of Iowa.

Fowler, L.T., and Jones, R. (1982). *Initial validation study, case classification and workload management system.* Springfield, Ill.: Illinois Department of Corrections.

Frisbie, L.V. (1969). *Another look at sex offenders in California.* California Mental Health Research Monograph, 12. Sacramento: Department of Mental Hygiene.

Gabor, T. (1986). *The prediction of criminal behaviour: Statistical approaches.* Toronto: University of Toronto Press.

Gendreau, P., Grant, B.A., and Leipciger, M. (1979a). Self-esteem, incarceration and recidivism. *Criminal Justice and Behavior, 6*, 67–73.

Gendreau, P., Madden, P.G., and Leipciger, M. (1979b). Norms and recidivism for first incarcerates: Implications for programming. *Canadian Journal of Criminology, 21*, 1–26.

Gendreau, P., Madden, P.G., and Leipciger, M. (1980). Predicting recidivism with social history information and a comparison of their predictive power with psychometric variables. *Canadian Journal of Criminology, 22*, 328–37.

Glueck, S., and Glueck, E. (1959). *Predicting delinquency and crime.* Cambridge, Mass: Harvard University Press.

Gottesman, I.I. (1991). *Schizophrenia genesis: The origins of madness.* New York: Freeman.

Gottfredson, D.M., Wilkins, L.T., and Hoffman, P.B. (1978). *Guidelines for parole and sentencing.* Toronto: Lexington.

Gottfredson, M.R., and Hirschi, T. (1990). *A general theory of crime.* Stanford: Stanford University Press.

Gottfredson, M.R., Mitchell-Herzfeld, S.D., and Flanagan, T.J. (1982). Another look at the effectiveness of parole supervision. *Journal of Research in Crime and Delinquency, 19*, 277–98.

Hare, R.E. (1991). *The Revised Psychopathy Checklist.* Toronto: Multimedia Health Systems.

Harris, G.T., Rice, M.E., and Quinsey, V.L. (1993). Violent recidivism of mentally disordered offenders: The development of a statistical prediction instrument. *Criminal Justice and Behavior, 20*, 315–35.

Hart, S.D., Kropp, P.R., and Hare, R.D. (1988). Performance of male psychopaths following conditional release from prison. *Journal of Consulting and Clinical Psychology, 56*, 227–32.

Heilbrun, A.B., Heilbrun, L.C., and Heilbrun, K.L. (1978). Impulsive and premeditated homicide: An analysis of subsequent parole risk of the murderer. *Journal of Criminal Law and Criminology, 69*, 108–14.

Hoffman, P.B. (1983). Screening for risk: A revised Salient Factor Score (SFS81). *Journal of Criminal Justice, 11*, 539–47.

Hoffman, P.B., and Beck, J.L. (1985). Recidivism among released Federal prisoners: Salient Factor Score and five-year follow-up. *Criminal Justice and Behavior, 12*, 501–07.

Holland, T.R., Holt, N., and Brewer, D.L. (1978). Social roles and information utilization in parole decision-making. *Journal of Social Psychology, 106*, 111–20.

Hughes, G., and Zamble, E. (1993). A profile of Canadian correctional workers: How they experience and respond to job stress. *International Journal of Offender Therapy and Comparative Criminology, 37,* 99–113.

Jackson, D.N. (1989). *Basic Personality Inventory.* London, Ontario: Research Psychologists Press.

Kazdin, A.E. (1987). Treatment of antisocial behavior in children: Current status and future directions. *Psychological Bulletin, 102,* 187–203.

Laws, D.R. (Ed.). (1989). *Relapse prevention with sex offenders.* New York: Guilford Press.

Lazarus, R.S., and Folkman, S. (1983). *Stress, appraisal, and coping.* New York: Springer.

Liberman, R.P. (1988). *Psychiatric rehabilitation of chronic mental patients.* Washington, D.C.: American Psychiatric Press.

Loeber, R., and Stouthamer-Loeber, M. (1986). Family factors as correlates and predictors of juvenile conduct problems and delinquency. In M. Tonry and N. Morris (Eds.), *Crime and justice,* vol. 7 (pp. 29–149). Chicago: University of Chicago Press.

Loucks, A., and Zamble, E. (1994) Some comparisons of male and female serious offenders. *Forum on Corrections Research, 6,* 22–5.

Loza, W., and Simourd, D.J. (1994). Psychometric evaluation of the Level of Supervision Inventory (LSI) among Canadian federal offenders. *Criminal Justice and Behavior, 21,* 468–80.

MacCulloch, M.J., Snowden, P.R., Wood, P.J.W., and Mills, H.E. (1983). Sadistic fantasy, sadistic behaviour and offending. *British Journal of Psychiatry, 143,* 20–9.

Malcolm, P.B., Andrews, D.A., and Quinsey, V.L. (1993). Discriminant and predictive validity of phallometrically measured sexual age and gender preferences. *Journal of Interpersonal Violence, 8,* 486–501.

Mandelzys, N. (1979). Correlates of offense severity and recidivism probability in a Canadian Sample. *Journal of Clinical Psychology, 35,* 897–907.

Marlatt, G.A., and Gordon, J.R. (1985). Relapse prevention: Theoretical rationale and overview of the model. In G.A. Marlatt and J.R. Davidson (Eds.), *Relapse prevention: Maintenance strategies in the treatment of addictive behaviors* (pp. 3–70). New York: Guilford Press.

Monahan, J. (1981). *Predicting violent behavior: An assessment of clinical techniques.* Beverly Hills, Calif.: Sage.

Motiuk, L.L., Bonta, J., and Andrews, D.A. (1986). Classification in correctional halfway houses: The relative and incremental predictive criterion validities of the Megargee-MMPI and LSI systems. *Criminal Justice and Behavior, 13,* 33–46.

Motiuk, L.L., and Porporino, F.J. (1989). *Offender risk/needs assessment: A study of conditional releases.* Ottawa: Solicitor General of Canada.

Motiuk, M.S., Motiuk, L.L., and Bonta, J. (1992). A comparison between self-report and interview-based inventories in offender classification. *Criminal Justice and Behavior, 19,* 143–59.

Nietzel, M.T., and Himelein, M.J. (1987). Probation and parole. In E.K. Morris and C.J. Braukmann (Eds.), *Behavioral approaches to crime and delinquency: A handbook of application, research, and concepts* (pp. 109–33). New York: Plenum Press.

Nuffield, J. (1982). *Parole decision-making in Canada: Research towards decision guidelines.* Ottawa: Supply and Services Canada.

Pithers, W.D., et al. (1988). Relapse prevention of sexual aggression. In R.A. Prentky and V.L. Quinsey (Eds.), *Human sexual aggression: Current perspectives* (pp. 244–60). New York: Annals of the New York Academy of Sciences.

Porporino, F., and Zamble, E. (1984). Some factors in the prediction of adaptation to imprisonment. *Canadian Journal of Criminology, 26,* 403–21.

Porporino, F.J., Zamble, E., and Higginbottom, S.F. (1990). Assessing models for predicting risk of criminal recidivism. Unpublished manuscript, Queen's University.

Quinsey, V.L. (1980). The baserate problem and the prediction of dangerousness: A reappraisal. *Journal of Psychiatry and Law, 8,* 329–40.

Quinsey, V.L. (1984). Institutional release policy and the identification of dangerous men: A review of the literature. *Criminologie, 17,* 53–78.

Quinsey, V.L. (1988). Assessments of the treatability of forensic patients. *Behavioral Sciences and the Law, 6,* 443–52.

Quinsey, V.L. (1995). The prediction and explanation of criminal violence. *International Journal of Law and Psychiatry, 18,* 117–27.

Quinsey, V.L., Coleman, G., Jones, B., and Altrows, I. (in press). Proximal antecedents of eloping and reoffending among mentally disordered offenders. *Journal of Interpersonal Violence.*

Quinsey, V.L., and Lalumière, M.L. (1995). Evolutionary perspectives on sexual offending. *Sexual Abuse: A Journal of Research and Treatment, 7,* 301–15.

Quinsey, V.L., and Maguire, A. (1986). Maximum security psychiatric patients: Actuarial and clinical prediction of dangerousness. *Journal of Interpersonal Violence, 1,* 143–71.

Quinsey, V.L., Reid, K.S., and Stermac, L.E. (1996). Mentally disordered offenders' accounts of their crimes. *Criminal Justice and Behavior, 23,* 472–89.

Quinsey, V.L., Rice, M.E., and Harris, G.T. (1995). Actuarial prediction of sexual recidivism. *Journal of Interpersonal Violence, 10*, 85–105.

Quinsey, V.L., and Walker, W.D. (1992). Dealing with dangerousnes: Community risk management strategies with violent offenders. In R.D. Peters, R.J. McMahon, and V.L. Quinsey (Eds.), *Aggression and violence throughout the life span* (pp. 244–62). Newbury Park, Calif.: Sage Publications.

Rhodes, W. (1986). A survival model with dependent competing events and right-hand censoring: Probation and parole as an illustration. *Journal of Quantitative Criminology, 2*, 113–37.

Rice, M.E., and Harris, G.T. (1995). Violent recidivism: Assessing predictive validity. *Journal of Consulting and Clinical Psychology, 63*, 737–48.

Rice, M.E., Harris, G.T., Quinsey, V.L., and Cyr, M. (1990a). Planning treatment programs in secure psychiatric facilities. In D. Weisstub (Ed.), *Law and mental health: International perspectives*, vol. 5 (pp. 162–230). New York: Pergamon Press.

Rice, M.E., Quinsey, V.L., and Houghton, R. (1990b). Predicting treatment outcome and recidivism among patients in a maximum security token economy. *Behavioral Sciences and the Law, 8*, 313–26.

Ross, R.R., Fabiano, E.A., and Ewles, C.D. (1988). Reasoning and rehabilitation. *International Journal of Offender Therapy and Comparative Criminology, 32*, 29–35.

Shover, N. (1996). *Great pretenders: Pursuits and careers of persistent thieves.* Boulder: Westview Press.

Siegel, J.M. (1986). The Multidimensional Anger Inventory. *Journal of Personality and Social Psychology, 51*, 191–200.

Skinner, H.A. (1982). Drug Abuse Screening Test. *Addictive Behaviours, 7*, 363–371.

Skinner, H.A., and Horn, J.L. (1984). *Alcohol Dependence Scale User's Guide.* Toronto: Addiction Research Foundation.

Spielberger, C.D., Gorsuch, R.L., and Lushene, R.E. (1970). *Manual for the State-Trait Anxiety Inventory ("Self-Evaluation Questionnaire").* Palo Alto, Calif.: Consulting Psychologists Press.

Steadman, H.J., and Cocozza, J.J. (1974). *Careers of the criminally insane: Excessive social control of deviance.* Toronto: Lexington Books.

Thornberry, T.P., and Jacoby, J.E. (1979). *The criminally insane: A community follow-up of mentally ill offenders.* Chicago: University of Chicago Press.

Villeneuve, D., and Quinsey, V.L. (1995). Predictors of general and violent recidivism among mentally disordered prison inmates. *Criminal Justice and Behavior, 22*, 397–410.

Waller, I. (1974). *Men released from prison*. Toronto: University of Toronto Press.

Webster, C.D., Harris, G.T., Rice, M.E., Cormier, C., and Quinsey, V.L. (1994). *The violence prediction scheme*. Toronto: Centre of Criminology, University of Toronto.

West, D.J., and Farrington, D.P. (1973). *Who becomes delinquent?* London: Heinemann.

Wormith, J.S., and Goldstone, C.S. (1984). The clinical and statistical prediction of recidivism. *Criminal Justice and Behavior, 11*, 3–34.

Zamble, E. (1992). Behavior and adaptation in long-term prison inmates: Descriptive longitudinal results. *Criminal Justice and Behavior, 19*, 409–25.

Zamble, E., and Porporino, F.J. (1988). *Coping, behavior, and adaptation in prison inmates*. New York: Springer.

Zarb, J.M. (1978). Correlates of recidivism and social adjustment among training-school delinquents. *Canadian Journal of Behavioural Science, 10*, 317–28.

Recidivism Project: Interview Form

[THIS IS THE VERSION used for recidivists; some questions differ for the control sample. A separate consent sheet contains the subject's name (with signature), FPS (RCMP identification number), and a subject number unique to the study; this is kept separately and securely, and subjects are identified in data files only by their study number.]

(Notes: Bridging dialogue is in italics, but questions are in normal text. Instructions are in parentheses. [Comments added for publication are in brackets.] Additional questions to clarify answers are always permissible. In general, answers should be recorded verbatim as much as possible, even if categories are supplied in the text, to allow later (re)categorization. However, the interviewer should keep possible categories in mind in seeking clarification.)

Introduction

As we explained before, what we are trying to do is to find out what is happening in men's lives while they are out on the street after being in prison. We are trying to find out what sorts of things happen before a new offence, so that in the future we might be able to predict recidivism or maybe even prevent it.

Given what we're interested in, you should be able to see why we're asking most of the questions that follow. If not, you can ask for an explanation, and I'll try to explain, although it may not be until we've finished the interview because it's very important that we finish in the time we have available. Also, if you have other information that you think is important that I don't ask about, please tell me. This is really the first time that anybody has tried to do this study, so we know it's not perfect.

The last thing I want to say before we get started is to remind you that you have the right to refuse to answer any particular question, although I'd appreciate your telling me why if there's anything you don't want to answer. Do you have any questions now?

Background

[Questions in this section are primarily intended to provide information for the LSI.]

Let me start with some general stuff. I want to know a bit about your background generally, so these questions do not apply to just the last time you were outside. This set of questions is sort of a grab bag, but I'm asking them all now because they may be hard to find in your file, and they may not fit anywhere else.

(1) How far did you go in school before you left? (Distinguish from upgrading in prison.)

(2) Were you ever suspended or expelled from school? (Y/N)

(3) How old were you when you left school?

(4) What was the reason you left? (Want to be able to characterize degree of interest and participation.)

(5) How well did you get along with the other students?
Very well
Satisfactorily
Not so well
Poorly

(6) How well did you get along with the teachers?
Very well
Satisfactorily
Not so well
Poorly

(7) How old were you the first time you ever got into trouble with the law?

(8) What's the longest time you've ever lived in the same place, since you've been on your own? (mos)

(9) What was the longest time you ever worked in the same job? (mos)

(10) Have you ever been fired from a job? (Y/N)

    (a) (If yes) Explain.

(11) What is the longest time you've ever lived with a woman? (mos)

(12) Have you ever had an alcohol or drug problem? (Y/N)

    (a) (If yes) When? (time before present)

    (b) At what age did your alcohol/drug use become a problem? Drug or alcohol use can cause a variety of problems for people. Did it cause problems for you in any of the following? (Regardless of answer, ask each of the following:)

No 0   Alcohol 1   Drugs 2   Both 3

    (i) Health (e.g., D.T.'s, liver)

    (ii) Family (fights with spouse, parents)

    (iii) Relationships with friends/others

    (iv) Legal (getting into trouble)

    (v) Employment/school

    (vi) Financial situation

    (vii) Other

(13) Even if you didn't have a problem, did other people ever say anything about your alcohol/drug use? (If yes, get details.)

(14) Have you ever been treated for an alcohol or drug problem? (Y/N)

(15) Have you ever had any problems that could have been treated by a psychologist or psychiatrist? (Y/N)

    (a) (If yes) Did you ever have treatment for it on the outside? (Y/N)

    (b) (If yes, get details: diagnosis, length, and type of treatment.)

    (c) Did you ever get any kind of treatment for emotional problems while you were in prison? (Y/N)

    (d) (If yes, get details: diagnosis, length, and type of treatment.)

(16) Have you ever seriously considered suicide? (Y/N)

(If yes)

    (a) When? (Time before present)

    (b) Did you actually attempt it?

General Problems

[This section and those that follow primarily deal with problems experienced, starting with open-ended questions and becoming more specific later. However, many of the questions provide information for the LSI and for other purposes.]

OK, let's move on to more recent things. What I am going to ask you about in most of the rest of my questions will focus on the period before your new offence, let's say mostly the last month. As much as possible, I'd like you to recall what was happening then, especially in the last few days before your new offence. Unless I tell you otherwise you should answer with what was happening around that time. Is that clear?

Let's start with a very general question. Were there any particular problems that you remember in the month before your offence? (If yes get specific descriptions. If no, repeat in a different form.)

Well, were there things that made your life difficult, or that you were having trouble dealing with? (Specify)

(Make sure that each of the general areas in the rest of the interview is covered. Questions that were answered in response to the general inquiry may be omitted.)

Well, we know from talking to other guys that there are a number of things that they often have trouble with. Let me ask you about them.

Accommodation

First, let's get some information about where you were living and who you were living with in the month before your last offence.

(1) So who were you living with? (Circle each one that applies, if changed during month.)

Nuclear family (wife, common-law, children)	1
Family of origin (parents)	2
Other family (siblings, aunt/uncle, cousins)	3
Friends	4
On your own	5

(2) What kind of place were you living in?

Own house/condominium	1
Rented house/apartment	2
Room	3
Shelter/hostel	4
Institution	5
No fixed address	6
Other (specify)	7

(3) Including that one, how many different places had you lived in during the previous year?

(4) Would you say that where you lived was in a high-crime neighborhood?

(5) What sort of problems did you see with your living arrangements?
Crowded
Poor condition
Other physical (noisy, location, etc.)
Interpersonal: neighbors
Interpersonal: living companions

(6) (If not already answered) Did you have any problems with the other people you were living with?
(If yes) What? (Specify)

(7) How about neighbors? Were there any problems with them?
(If yes) What? (Specify)

Supervision

(1) You were under supervision by a parole officer, right? (Y/N)

(2) What special terms were attached to your release, e.g., having to abstain from alcohol?

   (a) (If yes) When was the first time you broke any of those rules?

   (b) Was there anything that you can remember that was happening in your life at that time that might have led you to break your terms? (Generally want antecedents and consequences, here as well as elsewhere.)

   (c) Did your release terms create any difficulties for you?

(3) How well did you get along with your parole officer?

Excellent	1
Good	2

OK 3

Not so good 4

Poor, terrible 5

(4) Do you think that he/she helped you to get along on the outside, or did he/she maybe make no difference, or even make it harder for you? (Explain.)

(5) What could he/she have done differently so that you wouldn't be here today?

Financial Situation

I want to ask you now about your financial situation, still for the last month before the offence.

(1) What was your main source of income?

    Employment 1

    U.I.C. or disability 2

    Welfare 3

    Spouse/family 4

    Friends 5

    Illegal activities 6

    Other (specify) 7

(2) Did you have any money problems? (Specify)

(3) Were you able to make ends meet or were you running up debt?

(4) Did you have a bank account?

(5) How about credit: Had you borrowed any money from a bank or loan company, or anyone else? (If yes, get details.)

(6) Did you have a charge card or credit card?

(7) Did you have any debts that you couldn't pay, or have problems like checks bouncing or credit cards cut off?

Employment

Now I would like to ask you some questions about work during the period we're interested in.

(1) Were you working?

    (a) (If not working) Were you doing something else, like going to school?

Unemployed/not in school   1
Student (any program)   2
Employed full time   3
Employed part time   4

(2) How long had you been doing that?

(3) (If working) Was there any chance that you were going to lose your job?

(4) How well did you like your job (program)?

Very well   1
Somewhat   2
Neutral   3
Disliked some   4
Strongly disliked 5

(5) How did you obtain your job? (specify)

(a) On your own (newspaper, etc.)

(b) Through a friend

(c) Through an employment agency (specify)

(d) Other

(6) Would you say that you worked hard at it?

(7) Did you find it hard to get up every morning to go to work/school?

(8) How often were you late or absent?

(9) Were you having any problems with work/school?

(a) (If yes) What?

(10) (If not already answered) How well did you get along with your boss/teachers? Were there any problems there?

(a) (If yes) What? (Specify)

(11) How about with the other people you worked with (the other students/trainees)? How did you get along with them?

(a) (If any problems, specify)

Leisure/Recreation

All right, now I am interested in what you did in your spare time. Remember, we're still in that last month.

(1) What did you usually do in your spare time?
    (Try to specify activities within each category, and get number of hours/week.)

Ever? Hrs/wk

No Yes

(a) Family activities, including housework

(b) Hobbies/crafts

(c) Listening to music

(d) Watching TV

(e) Physical activities: sports/recreation

(f) Specific activities with friends

(g) Hanging around with friends

(h) Other (specify)

(2) How often did you feel bored?

Never	1
Rarely	2
Sometimes	3
Often	4
All the time	5

(3) Did you have enough friends?

(a) If you had a personal problem about something, could you go to them for help?

(b) Did you?

(c) (If no to either of the preceding) Why not?

(4) What sort of problems did you have with your friends?

Marital/Family Relationships

I want to ask now about family.

(1) During that last month, were you married or living with a woman? (Alternative questions may be used to arrive at classification below.)

Legally married	1
Common-law	2
Separated or divorced	3
Single	4
Other (specify)	5

(a) (If married) How well was the relationship working out?

(b) If you had a personal problem about something, could you go to her for help?

(c) Did you?

(d) (If no to either of the preceding) Why not?

(2) Even if you were satisfied with your marital arrangement, did it give you any problems?

(a) (If yes) What? (Specify)

How about other family relationships now?

(3) Were you in contact with your parents?

(a) How often did you see them or talk to them on the phone?

(b) Generally, how well did you get along with them?

(c) If you had a personal problem about something, could you go to them for help?

(d) Did you?

(e) (If no to either of the preceding) Why not?

(4) What sort of problems did you have with your parents?

(5) How about brothers and sisters? Do you have any?

(a) (If yes) How well did you get along?

(b) If you had a personal problem about something, could you go to them for help?

(c) Did you?

(d) (If no to either of the preceding) Why not?

(6) What problems, if any, did you have with your brothers and sisters?

(7) Has anyone else in your family been convicted of a criminal offence?

(If yes) Who?

Alcohol/Drug Use

All right, now I want to ask you a few questions about your use of alcohol and/ or drugs in the period I care most about, that is, in the last month.

(1) First, did you drink or use drugs during that time?

No 0   Alcohol 1   Drugs 2   Both 3

(2) How much did you drink on a usual drinking day?

Type   Standard drinks

(3) On how many days during that last month (week) did you drink your usual amount?

(4) Before that, how soon did you start drinking after your last release?

(5) Can you remember what led you to start drinking in that period?

(6) What drugs did you do?

(7) How often did you take (each of above)?

(8) On how many days during the last month (week) did you take your average amount of drugs?

(9) How soon after your last release did you start taking drugs?

(10) Can you remember what led you to start?

(11) How would you describe your behavior when you had been drinking? (Specify; check all below if not clearly stated in answer.)

    (a) Did you get into arguments or become verbally abusive?
        Never 1   Sometimes 2   Often 3   Most of the time 4
        Always 5

    (b) Did you become physically aggressive, violent?
        Never 1   Sometimes 2   Often 3   Most of the time 4
        Always 5

    (c) Did you become withdrawn, isolated, or moody?
        Never 1   Sometimes 2   Often 3   Most of the time 4
        Always 5

    (d) Did you ever become physically aggressive or violent when *not* drinking or using drugs?
        Never 1   Sometimes 2   Often 3   N/A 9   R/A 0

(12) Were you drinking in the 24 hours just before the new offence?

    (a) (If yes) How much?

    (b) For how many days in a row?

(13) How would you describe your behavior when you had been taking drugs? (Specify; include all below if not clearly stated in answer.)

    (a) Did you get into arguments, or become verbally abusive?
        Never 1   Sometimes 2   Often 3   Most of the time 4
        Always 5

    (b) Did you become physically aggressive, violent?
        Never 1   Sometimes 2   Often 3   Most of the time 4
        Always 5

    (c) Did you become withdrawn, isolated, or moody?
        Never 1   Sometimes 2   Often 3   Most of the time 4
        Always 5

(14) Did you take any drugs in the 24 hours just before the new offence?

   (a) (If yes) Which?

   (b) How much (of each)?

   (c) How many days in a row just before the offence?

(15) This may seem like a dumb question, but can you tell me why you were drinking/doing drugs?

   (a) Did you look forward to it when you weren't doing it?

   (b) What went through your mind when you thought about getting a drink/hit?

Emotional/Health Problems

(1) In that last month, did you have any problems with your feelings or moods?

   (a) (If yes) What?

   (b) (If yes) What was the problem, and what help did you get?

(2) During the whole month before your new offence, what kind of strong emotional feelings did you have? (Allow subject to respond freely, but cue if he does not respond. Inquire whether answers not on the list are equivalent to those that are, but do not force entries into our categories. After doing this, from set of all cited, get subject to specify which was the strongest one in each period.)

   (a) Hopelessness

   (b) Depression

   (c) Moody or brooding

   (d) Anger

   (e) Frustration

   (f) General stress

   (g) Anxiety/worry/fear

   (h) Guilt

   (i) Loneliness

   (j) Boredom

   (k) Sexual frustration

   (l) Felt nothing – numb

   (m) Positive/happy

   (n) Other

(3) How about in the 48 hours preceding the offence – what were you feeling then?

    (a) Hopelessness

    (b) Depression

    (c) Moody or brooding

    (d) Anger

    (e) Frustration

    (f) General stress

    (g) Anxiety/worry/fear

    (h) Guilt

    (i) Loneliness

    (j) Boredom

    (k) Sexual frustration

    (l) Felt nothing – numb

    (m) Positive/happy

    (n) Other

(4) Do you remember at all what set off those feelings? (Specify – we want sequence of actions, events, and thoughts.)

    (a) Did you do anything about it? (If yes) What?

(5) Were there any particular problems that were bothering you then, even some that we've already discussed?

    (a) Did you ever worry that your life wasn't going the way you wanted it to?

(6) How would you rate your life, on a scale of 1 to 100, where 1 is unbearable and 100 is all you'd ever want from life?

(7) Before you got into trouble, how confident were you that you could succeed on the outside?

Completely confident	1
Fairly confident	2
Halfway confident	3
A little lacking in confidence	4
Completely lacking in confidence	5

Offence Information

[After problems, finally to the offence. The majority of these questions provide information similar to that from the telescopic timeline, done later.]

Now I would like to ask you some specific questions about the offence. Remember that what we say is confidential.

(1) When did the thought of committing an offence like it first pass through your mind?
    (a) Had anything in particular happened to you just before that? (Specify)
    (b) (If no) Was there anything new that was happening in your life then, or some problem that was bothering you? (Specify)

(2) When you first thought about it, what did you do? (Specify)
    Ignore it or forget about it
    Thought about it a lot
    Started planning
    Acted on it
    (a) Did you try to resist the thoughts?
    (b) (If yes) How?

(The following questions may be omitted if obviated by answers to above, e.g., if he acted on first impulse.)

(3) Looking back at it now, when was the first time there was any serious chance that you might really commit an offence?
    (a) Were you aware at the time that something might be happening?
    (b) (If yes) What did you do about it?

(4) Did you ever daydream or fantasize about the offence before committing it?
    (a) (If yes) When was the first time?
    (b) How often? (Total frequency)
    (c) (If no) Why didn't you?
        Considered victim
        Worried about getting into trouble
        Just never happened
        Other
    (d) Did you ever think about all the good things that might come from it, e.g., respect from other guys, or lots of money, or maybe release from tension? (Specify)
    (For sex offenders only):
    (e) Did thinking about it get you sexually aroused?
    (f) Did you ever masturbate while you thought about it?

(g) (If yes) How often?

(h) Did you ever think about the bad things that might happen if you acted, e.g., return to prison? (Specify)

(5) Did you ever rehearse or make definite plans as to how you might carry out the offence?

    (a) (If yes) When did you start?

    (b) For how long altogether did you plan?

(6) Did you do your offence alone or with some other guys?

    (a) (If with others) Whose idea was it originally?

        Subject 1   Others 2

(7) What do you think really led you to do this offence?

Emotional state – general anger or frustration	1
Emotional state – specific anger, to get even	2
Emotional state – out of control, stressed out	3
Boredom, need for excitement	4
Need for money (day-to-day needs or other)	5
Sexual frustration or needs	6
Peer pressure	7
Just happened – never thought about it	8
Other (specify)	9

(8) Did you ever consider that you might be hurting somebody, that is, did you think of the victim?

    (a) (If yes) How often?

    (b) When did this first occur to you?

(9) Was there a point in the whole sequence where you could have stopped and just forgotten about the whole thing?

    (a) (If yes) Did it ever get to the point that you *weren't* in control any longer?

    (b) (If yes) When did it switch?

    (c) (If no) Does that mean that you were in control even at the end?

[Finally, to the timelines.]

OK, now we've probably covered just about everything. You can see that what we're trying to do is to get a picture of what was happening in your life before the offence, and how it all fits together. Now there might be things that you forgot to mention or that I didn't think to ask about, so I want to try to get a couple of real pictures.

First, I have here a sheet of paper with a timeline drawn on it. (Show.) As you can see, the endpoint here is the offence, and we've set it up this way to see how other things relate to it in time. We've drawn the line telescoped leading away from the offence, so you can see that near the end we have things divided in terms of minutes, and further back it's days or even months.

Now what I'd like you to do is to mark on the line when certain kinds of things happened. Some of these things may not have happened to you at all, and you can just tell me that instead of having to find a place for each event.

(10) Mark on the line:
   (a) First passing thought of offence
   (b) First time you thought about it for at least a minute
   (c) First time you considered that you *might* actually do it
   (d) First time you thought about details or means
   (e) First time you started definite planning
   (f) Point of no return – when it couldn't be stopped
(11) You can see I am trying to come up with some information to help me get an idea why you have come back here. Do you have any ideas yourself why you are here again?

You have indicated some problems in the areas of: (choose areas mentioned previously).

(12) For each problem area identified, how much did each of these difficulties bother you, i.e., how much were they a pain or hassle for you? (Use 1–10 ratings.)
   (a) Housing
   (b) Release supervision
   (c) Money
   (d) Work or educational program
   (e) Leisure time
   (f) Friends
   (g) Wife or family
   (h) Alcohol or drug use
   (i) Physical or emotional health

(13) *I have here another timeline, representing the month before the offence. You can see we have it marked off in days and weeks. I would like you to mark on the top line, the one called "events," any important things that were happening to you at the time, especially problems, including those we've just talked about. Then below, on the lines called "feelings" and "thoughts," I'd like you to mark what you remember about what you were thinking and feeling at those times. (Check that he understands, and demonstrate if necessary. Generally, the interviewer might do most of the actual writing on the timeline, as directed by the subject. At the end, the interviewer should compare the two timelines and attempt to establish correspondences and order of events, despite the differences in scaling.)* [The latter task proved too difficult and was abandoned after the first few subjects.]

(14) Now we've listed some of the problems you were facing in that period, and the order in which things happened. Do you think that these difficulties have anything to do with you committing your offence?

(If yes) How? (Specify)

Thank you, that's all of the questions that I have for you. Now, is there anything else that you can think of that might be important here that I haven't asked you about? [Very rarely any answers, but it probably helps to ask. After this, an arrangement is made about completion of questionnaires.]

Index